Tl and Avon

Lawrence Garner

Published by
Landmark Publishing
Ashbourne Hall, Cokayne Ave, Ashbourne,
Derbyshire DE6 1EJ England

The Severn and Avon

Shrewsbury

R. Severn Iron Bridge

Much Wenlock

Bridgnorth

CHAPTER 1

Kidderminster

Bewdley

Stourport

Droitwich

CHAPTER 2

Worcester

Malvern

CHAPTER 3

Upton-on-Severn

Bredon

Tewkesbury

Gloucester

Berkeley

CHAPTER 4

R. Avon

Pershore

Evesham

CHAPTER 7

Henley-in-Arden

Alcester

Stratford-on-Avon

CHAPTER 6

Kenilworth

Leamington Spa

Warwick

CHAPTER 5

Severn Estuary

N
W — E
S

0   5   10 miles

0   10km

Notes on the Maps

The maps drawn for each chapter, whilst comprehensive, are not intended to be used as route maps, but rather to locate the main towns, villages and points of interest. For exploration, visitors are recommended to use the 1:50,000 (approximately 1¼ inch to the mile) Ordnance Survey 'Landranger' maps. For walking, visitors are recommended to use the 1:25,000 (2½ inches to 1 mile) Ordnance Survey 'Explorer' and Outdoor Leisure maps.

Contents

Introduction   6

1. Shrewsbury to Bridgnorth   10
A Walk around Shrewsbury   12
On to Ironbridge   16
Across the river   22
On to Much Wenlock   22
A Tour of Remote Shropshire   24
Much Wenlock to Bridgnorth   29
A Walk around Bridgnorth   32
Places to Visit:
In and around Shrewsbury   34
In and around Ironbridge   35
In and around Much Wenlock   36
In and around Bridgnorth   37

2. Bridgnorth to Worcester   38
To Kidderminster   38
A Walk around Bewdley   41
A Walk around Stourport   44
Alternative Routes to Worcester   44
Via Witley Court   44
Via Harvington Hall & Droitwich   48
Droitwich   49
Places to Visit:
In and around Kidderminster   52
In and around Bewdley & Stourport 52
In and around Droitwich   53

3. Worcester and the Malverns   54
A Walk around Worcester   56
On to the Malverns   65

The Malverns   68
Great Malvern   68
A Walk around Great Malvern   69
Walking on the Malvern Hills   71
The Malvern Hills   73
A walk along the ridge   73
A Tour from the Malverns to   76
Upton-on-Severn
Places to Visit:
In and around Worcester   79
In and around Malvern   80-81

4. Upton-on-Severn to Gloucester 82
A Walk around Upton-on-Severn   84
On to Tewkesbury   85
A Walk around Tewksbury   88
On to Gloucester   90
Gloucester   92
A Walk around Gloucester   93
The Severn Vale   100
Places to Visit:
In and around Upton-on-Severn   103
In and around Tewkesbury   103
In and around Gloucester   103-04
In the Severn Vale   105

5. Leamington Spa,   106
Kenilworth & Warwick
A Walk around Leamington Spa   108
On to Kenilworth   110
Kenilworth   112
On to Warwick   112
A Walk around Warwick   113

On to Stratford-upon-Avon 117

Places to Visit:

In and around Leamington Spa 120

In and around Kenilworth 120

In and around Warwick 120-21

Places to Visit:

In and around Evesham 164-65

In and around Pershore 165

Factfile **166**

Index **174**

6. Stratford-upon-Avon and 122
the Warwickshire Countryside

A Walk around Stratford-upon-Avon 122

Exploring the Warwickshire 127
Countryside

Tour 1: South of Stratford-upon-Avon 127

Tour 2: Between Stratford 129
and Evesham

Tour 3: West to Alcester 133
and Coughton Court

A walk around Alcester 133

Tour 4: North to Henley-in-Arden 137

Places to Visit:

Stratford-upon-Avon 143

The four Warwickshire 144-45
Countryside Itineraries

Feature Boxes

The Roman City of Viroconium 17

The Ironbridge Gorge 20

Much Wenlock Priory 24

Bewdley 41

Stourport 43

Witley Court and Church 46

Worcester Cathedral 60

A walk on the Malvern Hills 71

Gloucester Docks 98

The Severn Bore 101

Joseph Arch of Barford 118

7. Evesham, Pershore and the 146
Worcestershire Countryside

Evesham 146

A Walk around Evesham 148

Exploring the Worcestershire 149
Countryside

Tour 1: Evesham to Pershore 149

Pershore/Walk around Pershore 156

Tour 2: South of Pershore 159
(a tour around Bredon Hill)

Introduction

There is a lot to be said for a holiday spent in following rivers. In themselves they create scenery that may be tranquil or exciting, but is seldom dull. Their effect on the lives of human beings has been profound, and the observant traveller is always conscious of the ingenious ways in which men have tried to use natural waterways to their own advantage, whether for energy, defence, irrigation, industry or transport. Riverside towns have an added dimension of interest and an enhanced visual attraction, and where bridges are few and far between the countryside flanking a river can remain remarkably unspoilt.

Opposite page: Gloucester
Left: Near the RSC, Stratford-upon-Avon
Below: Worcester Cathedral

In the case of the Severn and Avon there are added attractions arising from the contrast between them. From the point where it enters England west of Shrewsbury the Severn grows quickly into a formidable river, simultaneously a threat and an asset. It has always been a great commercial waterway – in the early nineteenth century cargoes were being hauled well into Wales, and until quite recently there was heavy traffic between Gloucester and Stourport.

The Avon has none of this drama. True, it served a valuable commercial purpose at one time, but that is distant history. Nowadays it follows a placid course, linking quiet towns and watering some of England's most peaceful and pastoral countryside. It is essentially a civilised river passing through a lived-in landscape.

Between them the two rivers shape the area covered by this guide. It is a rough triangle that includes much of

Top Tips

There is so much to explore that this list could easily be doubled with recommendations.

Stratford-upon-Avon
Shakespeare connections

Kenilworth Castle
Finest medieval palace buildings in country. Home of Robert Dudley – Elizabeth 1's favourite

Ironbridge Gorge Museums
Birthplace of the Industrial Revolution

Alcester
One of the most attractive small towns in England

Gloucester Cathedral
Largest stained glass window in England with the earliest example of fan vaulting (in the cloisters)

Tewksbury Abbey
One of the finest Norman towers in England

Worcester Cathedral
Houses the oldest royal effigy in England

Berkeley Castle
Where Edward 11 was murdered

Slimbridge Wildfowl Trust
Home of the Wildfowl and Wetlands Trust

Coughton Court (NT) & Witley Court (EH)
Two magnificent country houses.

Warwickshire and Worcestershire and substantial parts of Shropshire and Gloucestershire, providing a very happy balance between town and country. It comes as a surprise to find that this essentially rural area contains no fewer than three cities and nineteen major towns, all with distinctive characters and all worth exploring.

And what of the countryside? There is little point in supporting the publicity-writers' pretence that it is all 'beautiful'. Some of it is dull and some of it is spoilt. The orchards and market gardens of the Vale of Evesham, for example, have little visual appeal except during the short-lived 'blossom time'. The northern areas of Warwickshire and Worcestershire have been under heavy commuter pressure for a long time, and the result has been not only insensitive modern housing but also the cult of the picturesque which can transform ancient and unpretentious villages into potential film sets.

Fortunately it is still possible to find genuine countryside away from 'the world of tweed caps and Hush Puppies, headscarves and retrievers, purring Jaguars and glossy geldings', as one writer has memorably described it. In Shropshire, Worcestershire, Warwickshire and Gloucestershire a turn off the main road can lead to an unassuming world of small, close-knit communities that have always defined the character of the heart of England.

Suggestions for seeking out the best of the countryside are an essential part of this guide, which is written on the assumption that the average holidaymaker wants to squeeze a great deal of varied activity into a limited amount of time. For the same reason basic itineraries for each town are included. They are not intended to replace the excellent town trails that so many civic organisations now produce, but they will ensure that the visitor who has limited time, who finds the information centre unexpectedly closed or arrives in Stratford at 8am on a Sunday morning will be able to find the essential attractions.

Each chapter contains a subjective survey of a particular district, taking a fresh look at the well-known features and suggesting itineraries that include less famous but rewarding places. Occasional insets show outstanding attractions at a glance, and the final classified section is a comprehensive summary of what the area offers to visitors with a wide range of interests.

While the guide is written from the point of view of the land-based traveller it will obviously be of particular value to those planning a cruising holiday. The Severn is navigable for pleasure craft as far north as Stourport, and the Avon can be comfortably negotiated between Stratford and Tewkesbury. Canoeists, of course, have the freedom of both rivers.

Whatever the means of travel these two contrasting waterways and their surrounding countryside will provide the variety of experience that discerning visitors rightly seek.

Shrewsbury is the first English town on the River Severn. At a time when defence was a primary consideration it was inevitable that a settlement should grow up at this point, where the river describes a gigantic loop around a low hill and fails by only a few hundred yards to turn it into an island. With a castle sited to command the narrow strip of dry access, security was as strong as it could be in the violent Norman and early medieval period, when this border region rarely experienced tranquillity.

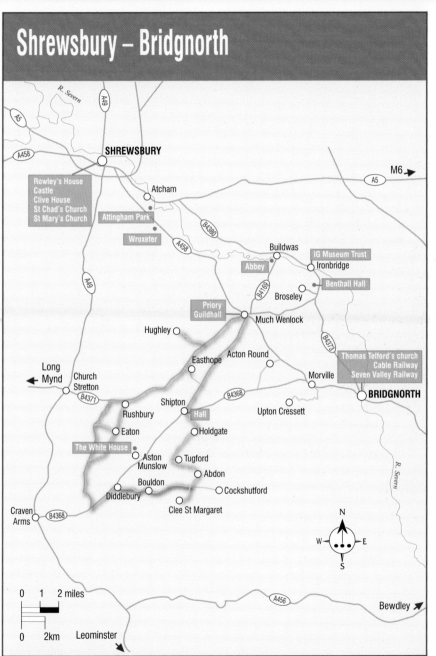

Shrewsbury – Bridgnorth

R. Severn

A5

A49

A458

A458

SHREWSBURY

M6

A5

Rowley's House
Castle
Clive House
St Chad's Church
St Mary's Church

Atcham

Attingham Park

Wroxeter

B4380

A458

A49

Buildwas

Abbey

IG Museum Trust

Ironbridge

Benthall Hall

B4169

Broseley

Priory
Guildhall

Much Wenlock

Hughley

Easthope

Acton Round

B4373

Thomas Telford's church
Cable Railway
Seven Valley Railway

Morville

Long
Mynd

Church
Stretton

B4371

Shipton

B4368

Upton Cressett

BRIDGNORTH

Rushbury

Hall

Eaton

Holdgate

The White House

Aston
Munslow

Tugford

Abdon

Bouldon

Cockshutford

R. Severn

Diddlebury

Clee St Margaret

Craven
Arms

B4368

N

W

E

S

0 1 2 miles

0 2km

Leominster

A456

Bewdley

Inevitably Shrewsbury became a military headquarters and administrative centre with a stability denied to other towns nearby, and although it had its share of problems they were never serious enough to inhibit steady economic growth. By the end of the thirteenth century, the town was the natural marketplace for a wide area of surrounding countryside and was beginning to develop a wool trade that was to be its main source of prosperity.

As a result, there is no Shropshire town that has a greater wealth of early buildings at its centre, and only Ludlow can match its standard of later development, particularly during the eighteenth century. Much has been lost, of course, through random clearance and rebuilding even in recent times, but enlightened conservation and a policy of putting old buildings to work for new commercial purposes have ensured that Shrewsbury remains a town of enormous interest without being a museum piece.

Traffic in a constricted space remains a problem, and you should never rely on finding a parking place. Visitors are advised to use the excellent park-and-ride service, which has three pick-up points clearly signposted off the approach roads. Since the buses stop at the **railway station** this is a convenient starting point for a tour of the town.

A walk around Shrewsbury

The **railway station** itself is worth looking at – a very grand nineteenth-century imitation of a stately home or Oxford college, befitting Shrewsbury's

former importance as a railway junction. Start climbing the hill that leads away from the station forecourt, and very soon you reach two notable buildings. On the right is the **library**, an impressive early seventeenth-century building that used to house Shrewsbury School; hence the statue in front commemorating Charles Darwin, one of its most distinguished former pupils.

Directly opposite is a lane leading to the **castle** (open to the public), which may prove something of a disappointment considering Shrewsbury's history as a military strongpoint. The earliest surviving remains are the eleventh-century perimeter walls and gateway. Edward I practically rebuilt the fortress in the late thirteenth century as a headquarters for his Welsh campaigns, and the Great Hall is the most substantial relic of that period. However, the castle now has a very civilised veneer as a result of Thomas Telford's remodelling in the late eighteenth century, when he converted it into a private house, thus paving the way for a distinguished early career as Shropshire's first County Surveyor.

Continue along Castle Street, where the big stores are the town's most obvious examples of nondescript modern development, although the smaller shops on the left-hand side retain an interesting variety of styles and facades. The point where the traffic turns into St Mary's Street was the site of the **High Cross**, where Henry Percy's body was displayed after the battle of Shrewsbury to dispel rumours that he was still alive. From here there is a view down the pedestrianised Pride Hill, a shopping street that has kept much of its lively character in spite of new buildings and reshaped shopfronts.

Turn into St Mary's Street, where the dominant feature is the large church occupying a pleasant square. The spire can hardly be appreciated from here but it is one of the tallest in England. Basically Norman, **St Mary's Church** has been extended and altered over centuries; one addition was the 1360 Chapel of the Drapers' Company, Shrewsbury's most powerful medieval guild. St Mary's is noted particularly for its rich collection of medieval stained glass, much of it gathered from Europe by a nineteenth-century incumbent, although the immense east window was transferred here from the old church of St Chad, which collapsed in 1788. The church is no longer used for worship, but is safely preserved and open to the public. St Mary's Place has on its south side the **Drapers' Hall**, built in the 1560s in affluent style with distinctively carved timbers.

Cross St Mary's Street and enter Church Street to find one of the town's most pleasant oases, **St Alkmund's Place**. The church of that name, on the south side, retains its medieval tower but otherwise is a reconstruction of 1794, notable for a superb Georgian east window and for the use of cast iron in its nave windows. St Julian's Church, just beyond it, has become redundant and is now a craft centre. The newly restored group of timber-framed buildings to the east is known as **Bear Steps**, and its outstanding feature is the fourteenth-century hall, used as an exhibition centre and normally open to the public. The roof timbers are particularly impressive. **Butcher Row** to the north

is a most picturesque street, dominated by the finely preserved Abbot's House at the top.

Descending steeply behind the Bear Steps, a steep and narrow alleyway (or 'shut' in these parts) with the graphic name of Grope Lane leads down into the High Street, where **The Square** can be seen immediately opposite. This is the old heart of the town, where the market was held for centuries; the sixteenth-century Market Hall still has its open ground floor and former courtroom above. The prominent statue is of Robert Clive, the Shropshire adventurer who enjoyed a meteoric career in India and returned to become MP for Shrewsbury in 1760. There is an interesting range of frontages on the north side of the Square but the most spectacular buildings in the vicinity are round the corner in High Street. **Owen's Mansion** and the even more splendid **Ireland's Mansion** face each other, both magnificent examples of the sort of ostentatious town house that the late sixteenth-century wool merchants could afford to build.

Walk up High Street to the point where it narrows at the top of the hill. From here the street known as **Wyle Cop** descends steeply towards the river. The **Lion Hotel** on the right is of immediate interest. At first glance it seems to be a typically handsome coaching inn of the eighteenth century, but downhill from the main entrance is a small wooden balcony that indicates a much earlier timber-framed structure. Just beyond it is the **Henry Tudor House**, a medieval shop with a fascinating upper window decorated with intricate tracery. Finally, near the

St Alkmund's church, Shrewsbury

Fish street, Shrewsbury

Charles Darwin statue, Shrewsbury

The Square, Shrewsbury

Shrewsbury Castle

bottom of the hill, the imposing **Mytton's Mansion** shows off its original opulence at first-floor level.

Wyle Cop leads on to the English Bridge and thence to **Shrewsbury Abbey** on its island site. It has become well known in recent years as the setting for Ellis Peters' *Brother Cadfael* novels. There was a Saxon church here, but the important monastic foundation was established by Roger de Montgomery in about 1080. At the dissolution of the monasteries in the sixteenth century the parishioners were allowed to keep the church, but the rest of the buildings quickly disappeared, the last remains being flattened when Thomas Telford drove his Holyhead Road through them in 1834, leaving only a refectory pulpit standing oddly on the far side of the road. The massive tower was added to the Norman nave in the fourteenth

century. Inside there is a marked contrast between the simplicity of this nave, with its huge pillars, and the richness of the chancel, which was sensitively restored in the 1880s.

Return over the bridge and take the road that branches to the left at the bottom of Wyle Cop. You soon come out onto the town walls high above the river, and into an area that is mainly eighteenth-century in character. The first notable building on the right is EW Pugin's **Roman Catholic Cathedral** of 1856, and not far beyond it Belmont is the first of several once-fashionable streets leading down to the town centre and providing an array of fine Georgian architecture.

An elegant vista now opens up ahead as the 'new' **St Chad's Church** comes into view. Standing on a prominent hill, St Chad's is the town's most striking church. The original St Chad's stood at the bottom of Belmont, and in 1788 Thomas Telford was called in to advise on its condition. He made himself unpopular by pronouncing it to be on the point of collapse. His report was ignored but shortly afterwards it did indeed fall down without warning. The task of building a new church was entrusted to George Steuart, who produced an imaginative design comprising a three-decker tower with cupola and entrance portico, with an antechamber leading to a circular nave capable of seating 2,000 people. The lightness and delicacy of the interior has been diminished a little by the addition of Victorian glass, but it is still a remarkable example of all that is best in eighteenth-century church architecture.

At this stage of the walk the riverside park opposite St Chad's, known as the **Quarry**, will no doubt be a welcome diversion, affording the chance to sit by the river or to visit the charming gardens created by the famous Percy Thrower and called the Dingle. There is talk of reopening this upper part of the river to navigation (boats could once be hauled well into Wales) and such a move would restore to Shrewsbury the enlivening water traffic that is such a cheerful feature of Severnside towns further south. Not that there is a lack of activity on the water; Shrewsbury is a leading rowing school and this stretch is used for training. Some of the extensive buildings now occupied by **Shrewsbury School** can be seen up on the opposite bank.

There is a short riverside walk from here to the Welsh Bridge, where you can cross the river to explore the ancient suburb of **Frankwell**, which has its own share of interesting buildings. Alternatively, return to St Chad's and walk down Claremont Hill on the far side of the church. It emerges into busy Barker Street, and by turning left you can reach **Rowley's House**, Shrewsbury's principal museum. It stands oddly amid a rather barren waste, but nothing can detract from the impact of this large timber-framed house with a stone-built mansion grafted on at the back, and recent refurbishing has enhanced its appeal. It is a further short walk to the Welsh Bridge, where the riverside walk will return you to your starting point at the railway station.

On to Ironbridge

To begin the journey down the Severn valley return to the Shrewsbury bypass (A5) and turn off onto the B4380 for Ironbridge. After 2m (3km) the river reappears on the left and passes under the road at **Atcham**, which is worth a stop. By parking in the lay-by on the right just before the bridge, you can see that there are in fact two bridges here, separated by only a few yards. The 'new' one dates from 1929 and is a rather elegant, balustraded affair, while the other, now closed to traffic, was built in about 1770 and has a much more rustic look. A 'Telford' milestone at its western end is the only indication that it once carried the Holyhead Road.

From the old bridge it is possible to admire the pleasing river frontage to the south provided by the mellow Georgian hotel and the sandstone church, which is the only one in the country dedicated to St Eata. Much of the north wall is

Saxon work, built with stones 'liberated' from the nearby Roman town of Viroconium. The dull exterior gives no indication of the riches inside. The east window, for example, is medieval glass, pale brown and gold, brought here from Bacton church in Herefordshire. There is a Tudor window in the north wall commemorating a lady-in-waiting to Elizabeth I. The fine carving on the vicar's stall dates from the sixteenth century. The general impression is sombre, partly because of the inward-leaning walls and heavy roof timbers and partly because of a simple lack of windows.

On the other side of the main road is the impressive entrance to **Attingham Park**, one of Shropshire's greatest houses. Originally built between 1783 and 1785, it was altered by John Nash in 1807 but still retains its classical symmetry. Humphrey Repton landscaped the elaborate grounds. The house and grounds are now owned by the National Trust and are open to the public.

The B4380 follows the park boundary for a long time before branching right just opposite an old tollhouse. After half a mile watch out for the car park on the right for visitors to the site of **Viroconium**.

The site looks small and a little unkempt, since excavation continues all the time, but what is seen on the surface is only a fraction of what remains to be unearthed. Most of the visible remains are of the extensive bath area, including a remarkably high section of wall, and the outline of the basilica, or public meeting place. The site museum is fascinating. The more precious finds are in the Rowley's House Museum in Shrewsbury, but equally interesting are the ordinary domestic objects shown here, including a meat cleaver and manicure set complete with nail file. Aerial photographs on display show, by means of crop marks, the outlines

The Roman City of Viroconium

At its height Viroconium was the fourth largest Roman city in Britain. Begun as a military camp on Watling Street in about AD50, it was developed as a civil town forty years later for the benefit of the native tribal people, the Cornovii. After desultory progress, work was accelerated as a result of the Emperor Hadrian's visit to Britain in AD125, and one of the great finds here was a big inscribed tablet recording the dedication of the forum to the Emperor. Sophisticated archaeological techniques have detected various disasters, among them the collapse of the forum colonnade, the stumps of which can be seen on the other side of the lane to Wroxeter. There is evidence that after the departure of the Romans, extensive wooden buildings were erected on the site, and a visit to nearby Wroxeter church will show that the stone was not wasted; the church gate boasts a Roman column on each side. It appears that Viroconium was never attacked; it was simply abandoned by its Romano-British occupants.

The Roman remains at Wroxeter above and top left opposite

of whole streets, houses and defence works beneath the surface of the adjacent farmland.

From here the B4380 continues over a high plateau with a splendid view of the Wrekin, Shropshire's trademark hill, on the left and the Welsh hills to the right. Another panorama opens up after the village of Leighton, when the road starts to run high above the Severn. Lay-bys provide a chance to stop and look at the river meandering dramatically below on its way to the entrance of the Ironbridge Gorge, marked by the cooling towers of a large power station. The next village is **Buildwas**, and to reach its famous abbey, take the next turning on the right towards Much Wenlock. The path to the abbey is 100yd (91m) past the river bridge.

Buildwas Abbey was founded in 1135 as a daughter house of Furness Abbey in Cumbria, and the original occupants were Savignacs (later Cistercians). The most substantial remains are of the church, with two finely proportioned nave arcades and the east and west window spaces still intact. Of the other buildings, the most impressive is the elaborately vaulted chapter house floored with medieval tiles. It is a most tranquil spot, which seems to get few visitors.

Return to the B4380 and continue down the hill. The immense cooling towers of the Buildwas power station dominate the scene ahead, and are quite possibly the most awe-inspiring sight in Shropshire. They are not inappropriate for this area, for you are now entering **Ironbridge**, once renowned for technological innovation – indeed the road signs proclaim this to be 'The Birthplace of Industry' – but now famous for its vast range of museums.

Buildwas Abbey, top right and below

The Ironbridge Gorge

It is probably no exaggeration to say that the course of civilisation was changed in this 4m (6km) length of the Severn. The basic reason was the concentration in a small area of timber, coal, ironstone, clay and limestone, with the river as a convenient means of transporting heavy products over long distances, but these natural advantages might have counted for little without their exploitation by a few men of vision.

The mining of coal and the production of iron in charcoal funaces was already expanding when Abraham Darby I arrived here in 1708 from Bristol. He was in the business of making iron cooking pots, but he was obsessed with the possibility of making thinner sheet iron and much bigger castings. He chose a site in Coalbrookdale, a valley running north from Ironbridge, and set about experimenting with the use of coke rather than charcoal for fuelling the furnaces. It was not an overnight breakthrough – several years passed before he was producing iron in large quantities by the new method – but the high quality of his product made possible developments that had been unthinkable before. The production of iron rails, for example, solved many transport problems and led to the rapid expansion of the industrial area.

It was Abraham Darby III who was responsible for the most spectacular pioneering achievement with iron. The lack of a river bridge had always been a problem, since coal and raw materials from Broseley on the other side had to be laboriously ferried across a difficult stretch of the Severn. The local ironmasters commissioned Darby to construct an iron bridge. Using entirely new engineering principles and making castings of an unprecedented size and weight, he completed the job in 1779. The bridge still stands, having given its name to the riverside settlement, and it has now become the symbol of the industrial achievements of the Gorge.

There were other achievements too. Thomas Telford came here to investigate the use of cast iron for canal aqueducts, and the eventual result was his remarkable structure at Pontcysyllte, near Llangollen. Richard Trevithick's innovative steam locomotive was developed in Coalbrookdale. On the Broseley side of the river John Wilkinson first applied steam power to iron production and produced the world's first iron boat. At the other end of the Gorge a thriving ceramics industry developed. Two major firms of tile manufacturers emerged at Jackfield, while the famous Coalport works produced some of the finest china ever made.

Inevitably the depletion of resources and the rapid exploitation of the new processes in other parts of the country led to a decline in the Gorge's industrial activity. The works were run down or abandoned and the population moved to seek work elsewhere. Since no one was interested in developing the area it remained fossilised, so in the 1960s the Ironbridge Gorge Museum Trust was able to set about creating the country's largest museum, now a World Heritage Site.

There is little point in describing the Ironbridge museum sites in detail since literature is so freely available, but it is worth pointing out that there is a passport ticket available for all the sites (a family ticket for parents and up to five children is a particular bargain) and the various portions can be used over a twelve-month period. It takes at least two days to explore everything thoroughly, and if only one site can be visited, the best choice for families is probably the child-friendly **Blists Hill**, which has a wide variety of exhibits in an open-air display, including a re-creation of a Victorian shopping street.

The following itinerary is suggested for those with limited time who want to catch the atmosphere of the Gorge. On entering the town from Buildwas take the first major road to the left, signposted **Coalbrookdale**. The road passes several restored buildings, including the magnificent Coalbrookdale Institute, and at the top of the hill you can park at the **Museum of Iron**, where Abraham Darby's original blast furnace has been preserved inside a striking modern building. A short walk in this area provides a chance to look at the remarkable variety of buildings, with ironmasters' elegant houses and workers' cottages planted haphazardly together.

On returning to the riverside turn left and almost immediately right into the car park of the **Severn Warehouse**, an odd Gothic building that looks like a chapel. It houses displays introducing the Gorge and its history. From here it is a short walk to the **iron bridge**, along a waterfront that has changed very little – a random mixture of cottages, pubs

and warehouses. The bridge is open only to pedestrians, and it is possible to get down to the riverbank beneath it to study the elaborate castings used in its construction. The town's shopping centre is on the other side of the road, with a harmonious line of shops leading down to the wharf and an attractive square. The most prominent building here is the handsome **Tontine Hotel** of 1778.

As you look at the town from the bridge its character becomes clear. It is built on a steep slope, on which houses in a variety of styles and sizes perch, laid out in no discernible plan. A quick exploration can start with the climb to St Luke's church. It may be your only chance to walk under a graveyard, since the top section of the climb is a tunnel formed when the churchyard was built over the top. To the west of the church a lane leads sharply downwards and will lead back to the waterfront. It provides unusual views of the houses below, and there are occasional glimpses of mysterious tracks leading off into the undergrowth. The idea of a preserved town sounds artificial, but the Trust seems to take a pride in retaining the original appearance of their dwellings, including the grimy brickwork and waste spaces.

You should now drive past the bridge and take the Broseley road at the little roundabout. Ignore the actual turn for Broseley and continue along a surprisingly rural lane to a T-junction. A left turn here goes to Blists Hill open-air museum. Continuing to Coalport in the other direction, you will pass the Shakespeare Inn, beyond which is a roadside parking area. Stop here and go down one of the paths opposite the pub to reach the foot of the **Hay inclined plane**, a notable feat of engineering designed to haul boats bodily up and down between the two levels of the canal. Here also is the **Tar Tunnel** (occasionally open), mined as a natural source of bitumen. The footbridge across the river at this point gives access to the **Jackfield Tile Museum**, which not only tells the story of the industry but also houses artisan workshops. The canal towpath leads to the **Coalport China Museum**, a treasure house of beautiful ceramics.

Across the river

Return the way you came, and this time take the Broseley road across the narrow bridge, which dates from 1908 and is of some interest as the first of any size to be constructed in reinforced concrete. On the other side of the river the road winds up adventurously with one very severe hairpin bend and enters **Broseley**. Take the first on the right after the garage to reach the old town and park at the church entrance.

The church is Victorian, impressively battlemented and decorated with large gargoyles. It stands on the edge of a steep hill with wide views across the river, and although there is nothing outstanding about the interior it conveys a sense of solidity and wealth. The famous ironmaster John Wilkinson was the eighteenth-century 'King' of Broseley, and his house, The Lawns, stands almost opposite the church with a prominent bow window which no doubt helped him to keep an eye on the main street. A walk further along Church Street and up into the shopping centre reveals a wealth of charming cottages and larger houses in a variety of appealing styles. The industrial grime has gone, and the little square could stand comparison with many a Cotswold village.

On to Much Wenlock

It is possible to reach **Benthall** this way (it is signposted about a mile out of town). **Benthall Hall** (mainly Elizabethan) is now a National Trust property, and the small church should not be missed. Although it appears to stand in the Hall grounds it was not a private chapel, but served a sizeable settlement here until the population was drawn away to the nearby centres of industry. The sundial over the door catches the eye outside, and the immaculate interior has box pews and a striking gilded monument in the sanctuary.

From here the road goes on to **Much Wenlock**, one of Shropshire's pleasantest small towns, boasting the ruins of a magnificent priory. Bypassed by the main road, the town's narrow streets are quiet and full of harmonious architecture. At the top end of the High Street beside the A458 is the extremely handsome Gaskell Arms, and the short walk back towards the town centre reveals several interesting buildings. Ashfield Hall has a stone ground floor supporting timber-framed upper works, while almost opposite a fine black and white house serves as Barclays Bank. Raynald's Mansion is one of the county's best Tudor town houses, with a carved facade and tiny balconies between its three gables. At the heart of the town is the beautifully preserved Guildhall,

The Priory (above) and The Guildhall (below), Much Wenlock

Much Wenlock Priory

The ruins of the Priory are extensive and represent the third set of monastic buildings on the site. The original foundation took place in the seventh century by the Mercian King Merewalh for his daughter Milburga, who wished to establish a monastic community. Some 200 years later Leofric of Mercia rebuilt it. After the Norman conquest Roger de Montgomery started the final ambitious scheme of construction, and it was during these works that the body of St Milburga, who had inspired several local legends, was reputedly discovered 'sound and uncorrupted'. At the sixteenth-century Dissolution of the Monasteries the Prior's lodging fell into private hands and remains intact today. Otherwise the ruins include substantial remains of the huge church, a finely decorated chapter house and the wellhead of the monks' lavatorium, which bears two imaginative pictorial carvings.

which still has its open ground floor and an upper room of great charm. The small but lively museum stands on the opposite corner.

The road from here to the Priory passes the parish church, of Norman origin but rather nondescript now. The severity of the Victorian restoration has been lightened somewhat by the recent refurbishing of St Milburga's Chapel in a striking contemporary style. Note also the memorial at the west end to Dr William Penney Brookes, a nineteenth-century athletics enthusiast and pioneer of the modern Olympic Games.

At the point where the path to the Priory branches off there is a group of very attractive old cottages, but the best blend of architecture in the town is in Shineton Street, which starts here. The range of houses and cottages in local stone have obviously been the subject of thoughtful conservation, and the unpretentious result is a triumph.

The A458 will take you quickly on to Bridgnorth, but visitors with time available may like to explore some of the finest and least spoilt countryside in Shropshire lying to the west of Much Wenlock. It includes Wenlock Edge, Apedale and Corvedale, and is rich in tiny hamlets, deserted villages and traces of mining and quarrying associated with the Clee Hills. The area repays leisurely exploration on foot, but it is possible to catch much of its atmosphere in the course of an afternoon's drive.

A tour of remote Shropshire

Leave Much Wenlock on the A458 (for Shrewsbury) and after half a mile (1km) turn left onto the B4371, which runs along **Wenlock Edge**, the long escarpment immortalised by the poet AE Housman (for walkers the Jack Mytton Way runs the length of the Edge). For the first mile or so the road runs between quarries producing the limestone that gives so many of the buildings in the area their distinctive look. Watch out for a concealed right fork after 2m (3km). It leads to **Hughley** by way of a steep road through the thick woodland that blankets the Edge. Hughley is a good example of the many isolated hamlets in this part of Shropshire, consisting mainly of farms and associated cottages, with the occasional 'big house'. The church is notable for its rare fifteenth-century chancel screen with some medieval floor tiles behind it.

As you return to the B4371 you appreciate the massive, barrier-like appearance of the Edge, which looks almost insuperable from below. Turn right, and after less than a mile lay-bys on each side of the road provide a chance to park and walk to one of the best viewpoints, with a panorama of thousands of acres of rich farmland, and the Wrekin rising sharply from it to the east.

Half a mile (1km) further on the Plough Inn marks a left turn down into Hopedale and the village of **Easthope** (walkers will note that a mile (1½km) beyond the Plough is the start of a fine walk along the top of the Edge to Eaton). Easthope is rather like Hughley in character but not in appearance, because here the cottages, barns and walls are built in the grey local stone. The church is isolated, but its site in the middle of lush green meadowland must be one of the most beautiful in the county. It was rebuilt after a fire in the 1920s, but has been faithfully restored, with a new chancel screen made from ancient timber. Perhaps the most interesting feature here is under a yew tree on the north-eastern side of the churchyard: two graves, uninscribed but with plain crosses, lie side by side, reputedly the resting-places of two monks who died in a drunken brawl.

After turning round take the left

Eaton Church

Easthope Church (above) and Wilderhope Manor, Youth Hostel, open to the public at certain times (below)

Diddlebury (above) and Rushbury (below)

turn at the junction near the church and rejoin the main road, which runs high and straight for 2m (3km) before emerging from the woodland and descending to Longville. After a further 2m (3km) look for an insignificant turn to **Rushbury**. A superb timber-framed house marks the outskirts of the village, and as you climb the hill to the centre there is an even better one on the left. Outstanding in a different style is the Old Rectory, a most ecclesiastical-looking building. The interior of the church is a huge rectangle with no obstructions, and is made even more imposing by heavy roof timbers.

Return to the road junction outside the village and turn left. The prominent hills ahead are part of the group to the east of Church Stretton. Turn left again opposite the farmyard just before the main road and drive for a little over 2m (3km) until you pass through the abutments of an old railway bridge that used to carry the line from Much Wenlock to Craven Arms. Just beyond it is **Eaton-under-Heywood**, a picturesque cluster of buildings tucked away beneath the Edge and almost smothered by the thick woodland above. The church of St Edith is one of the most interesting in Shropshire, with a good deal of untouched Norman work and a floor that slopes sharply up towards the altar. The original roof timbers and chancel ceiling are particularly fine, as is the Jacobean pulpit and canopy. The effigy lying within the sanctuary dates from the mid-fourteenth century.

As you drive away from Eaton, take the turning on the left just before the railway bridge. This is the start of the most remote and attractive part of the tour, starting under the shadow of the Edge and then gradually climbing it through magnificent woodland and isolated hamlets. The route is via Harton and Westhope and then through Seifton Batch, a deeply cut valley. The lane eventually joins the B4368, where you turn left and drive along a high road with views of Shropshire's most impressive range, the Clee Hills. Pass through Corfton and on to **Diddlebury**. The 'new' village lies beside the main road but the original centre is a few hundred yards down a side road, and very picturesque too with its stream and footbridge just below the church. This is very old indeed – its Saxon nave has herringbone masonry, there is a Saxon doorway, and the windows contain fourteenth-century glass.

Continue on the minor road past Diddlebury church and out into open country. Soon after crossing the River Corve, you pass some mounds in a field on the right, all that remains of Corfham Castle, once strategically sited to command the valley route. Pass through Peaton and into **Bouldon**, which was once an industrial village, with iron being produced here until the 1790s. The site was then converted for paper manufacture and finally became a corn mill in the 1840s.

From Bouldon the lane contines uphill to **Heath**, where Heath Chapel, standing isolated in its field, is on the left (if you want to go inside drive on about 300yds (274m) to the next farm for the key). This is a famous church because the shell has been almost untouched since it was first built in the eleventh century. Its door, font and chancel arch are fine examples of primitive Norman work, while the pews and other woodwork date from no later than the seventeenth century. In the neighbouring field the traces of the medieval village which it served are still visible.

At the next crossroads go straight on towards Cockshutford. At the top of a short steep hill is a lay-by from which it is possible to climb **Nordybank**, the Iron Age hillfort nearby. This area is part of the old Clee Hills mining district and is notable for the squatters' settlements carved out of the common land by miners. A track leads east from Nordybank onto the hills, and by following the ridge northwards walkers can reach the 1,700ft (518m) summit at **Abdon Burf**.

From the lay-by turn back to the crossroads and turn left for **Clee St Margaret**. The houses here have been thoroughly restored and its most interesting feature is the fact that one of the village streets is the Clee Brook, forming what is probably Britain's longest ford. To the north of Clee St Margaret is **Abdon**, a hamlet with an unusual history: the original medieval village became deserted and the place was virtually recolonised from the seventeenth century onwards by miners. The same thing happened at **Tugford**, 1½ m (3km) to the west, but here the squatters' cottages built on the village green were later demolished by order of the manor court, which explains why the church now stands alone in a field. There is a fine Norman doorway here, and fifteenth-century carving on the choir screen.

The way out of Tugford is signposted Stanton Long and runs across a high, windswept plateau, reaching **Holdgate**

after 3m (5km). This is another example of a 'failed' village. Once a major settlement, it now has only a motte and a stone tower incorporated into a house as reminders of its medieval importance, although the church has a notable Norman door and font. **Shipton** is the last stop on this itinerary. After passing through Stanton Long and reaching the outskirts of the village, go straight over at the first crossroads and turn left at the next junction to reach **Shipton Hall**. It is a handsome building dating from 1587, although the interior was altered a good deal in the eighteenth century, being equipped with iron fireplaces from Coalbrookdale. The open space in front of the Hall was created by clearing the existing village when it was built, although the little church was undisturbed and now perches on a nearby hill within the boundary of the Hall grounds.

The B4378 out of Shipton leads back to Much Wenlock, concluding a tour that has taken in some of the unfrequented countryside that typifies, if anything can, the essential character of Shropshire.

Much Wenlock to Bridgnorth

After leaving Much Wenlock on the A458 for Bridgnorth it is worth stopping at **Morville** to walk down to the church and survey the imposing facade of **Morville Hall**, an eighteenth-century mansion in grey stone flanked by substantial twin lodges. It is a National Trust property but can be inspected by written appointment only. The church has exceptional medieval

The iron bridge, Ironbridge

China Museum, Coalport

Jackfield Tile Museum

The Town Hall, Bridgnorth

The Castle remains, Bridgnorth

ironwork on the door, and the font and chancel arch are Norman. Four early wooden carvings of the Evangelists are placed at the top of the nave arcades.

And so into **Bridgnorth**, the most dramatic of the Severnside towns. The town centre is confusing for drivers unfamiliar with it. It is a good idea to ignore the first indicated turn for Bridgnorth off the A458 and continue on the bypass over the first roundabout until you cross the river. Then turn left and look for the car park on the left. From here it is a short walk to the main river bridge, which is a good starting point for a tour of the town.

To understand Bridgnorth you need to stand at the centre of the bridge. On the west bank of the river **High Town** perches on top of precipitous sandstone cliffs, and it is easy to see why it was selected as a castle site early in the twelfth century. Below the cliffs is the waterfront, the source of the town's second lease of life in the sixteenth century. Here, and continuing on the east bank, is **Low Town**, which acquired much of the more recent development. This very distinctive geography has ensured that High Town and Low Town have traditionally regarded themselves as independent communities.

A walk around Bridgnorth

The waterfront buildings are concentrated at the west end of the bridge, facing the landscaped remains of the wharves, and climbing away from them is a narrow street called the **Cartway**, for centuries the only way up the cliffs for wheeled vehicles. At the bottom of the Cartway it is impossible to miss

Bishop Percy's House, a splendid sixteenth-century structure with decorated timber-work. Apart from his ecclesiastical career the Bishop is best remembered for his collection of traditional ballads called *Reliques of Ancient English Poetry*, a volume that brought new vision to poets at the end of the eighteenth century and certainly inspired Sir Walter Scott.

The Cartway rises steeply, passing some quaint buildings, including a cave in the rock that was inhabited until 1856, and emerges at the south end of the **High Street**. The general effect of this wide thoroughfare is often masked by ranks of parked cars, but it is a pleasant, bustling shopping centre with many half-timbered buildings, notably the Swan Inn on the right. The **Town Hall** of 1652 is planted firmly in the middle of the street with traffic passing beneath it, and immediately after it Church Street leads off to the right towards the small 'close' surrounding **St Leonard's Church**.

This is a very attractive place indeed. The church itself (disused, but conserved and open to visitors) is Victorian, although its sandstone still looks remarkably new. Among the buildings grouped around it is the house occupied by **Richard Baxter** when he was a young curate here in the early 1640s and before he went on to become a controversial Puritan preacher and writer. The old Grammar School stands isolated nearby. On the other side of the green is **Palmer's Hospital**, a group of almshouses built round a tiny courtyard, with three fine seventeenth-century houses almost next door.

Back in the High Street, the **North-**

gate is the only survivor of the town's five medieval gates, although it has lost most of its character after extensive rebuilding. On the way back towards the town centre you pass Whitburn Street on the right, and a short way down is a very fine half-timbered pub called the King's Head. The Crown, at the corner of Whitburn Street, was once Bridgnorth's principal coaching inn.

There could hardly be a building less in keeping with its neighbours than the **New Market** at the south end of the High Street. Mid-Victorian, and constructed with bilious brick in Italianate style, it stands gloomily dwarfing the small-scale architecture around it. For a complete contrast cross the road into **East Castle Street**, Bridgnorth's most elegant road, where the predominantly Georgian houses fit harmoniously together with a distinct atmosphere of wealth. Thomas Telford's church of **St Mary Magdalene** closes off the end in a fitting classical fashion.

Visitors are always guaranteed a shock on taking the path to the rear of St Mary's and seeing the **castle keep** for the first time. It is a huge square block of masonry leaning at an incredible angle, the only substantial remnant of a Norman structure that once filled the site now laid out as a public garden. It can also be a surprise to hear the unmistakable sound of a steam train, but Bridgnorth is the northern terminus of the restored Severn Valley Railway, and there is a good view of the station and yards from the parapet here.

To reach the railway it is necessary to get to the bottom of the cliffs. The short way is to go back past the castle keep and turn left onto a flight of steps at the bottom of which are two terraces of highly individual workmen's cottages in Ebenezer Row and Railway Street. The station entrance is immediately opposite. However, the longer way round via the town centre provides a chance to travel on Britain's only inland **cliff railway** – a convenient link between High Town and Low Town that has served a useful purpose since Victorian times. The descent brings you out onto the wharf, and the walk to the station passes some of the caves in the cliffs that were once storehouses and dwellings.

This rapid survey hardly does justice to a town that is full of surprises and has a centre hardly affected by contemporary development. It seems entirely fitting that the visitor should be able to leave on a train of the Great Western or London Midland, both of which are represented among the locomotives and rolling stock of the **Severn Valley Railway**. The SVR started in 1965 as a small volunteer group, formed to revive the disused Bridgnorth to Worcester line, and by 1974 trains were running between Bridgnorth and Bewdley, a particularly attractive run that follows the river closely and includes some atmospheric rural stations. The line was later extended to Kidderminster. Over the years a very large collection of engines, carriages and wagons has been acquired and restored, and the SVR is now the largest of Britain's standard-gauge preserved lines.

Places to Visit

IN AND AROUND SHREWSBURY

Visitor Information Centre

The Music Hall, off The Square
☎ 01743 281200

In Shrewsbury

St Mary's Church

Medieval church noted for its spectacular Jesse window and medieval stained glass from various English and European sources.

St Chad's Church

Outstanding example of late 18th-century ecclesiastical architecture.

The Castle

☎ 01743 361196
Norman walls and gatehouse, later additions by Edward I converted by Thomas Telford into a private house. Now houses the Shropshire Regimental Museum.

Rowley's House

☎ 01743 361196
Impressive timber-framed building, now Shrewsbury's principal museum and art gallery. Includes discoveries at Roman town of Viroconium.

The Quarry

Riverside park and gardens, designed by famous BBC gardening expert Percy Thrower.

Coleham Pumping Station

Longden Coleham
☎ 01743 361196
Built 1896–1901 as part of town's sewerage system. Two beam-engines on view.

Bear Steps

Off St Alkmund's Place
Restored group of medieval buildings, with notable Hall used as exhibition room.

Market Hall

The Square
☎ 01743 281281
Built 1596 for the Drapers' Guild. Now a digital media centre with cafe.

Further afield

Viroconium (English Heritage)

Off B4380, 5 miles (8km) SE of Shrewsbury
☎ 01743 761330
Excavated site of Roman town at Wroxeter. Visitor centre on site. Adjacent church is of interest.

Wroxeter Vineyard

Adjacent to Viroconium
☎ 01743 761888
Award-winning wine producers. Shop.

Attingham Park (National Trust)

At Atcham, on B4380, 4m (7km) SE of Shrewsbury
☎ 01743 708123

Outstanding mansion of late 18th and early 19th centuries. Fine furniture and decoration, pictures and landscaped park.

Battlefield Church

On A49, 2m (3km) from northern edge of town

Interesting collegiate church built on site of Henry IV's victory over rebels in 1403.

Haughmond Abbey (English Heritage)

Off B5062 2m (3km) E of Shrewsbury
☎ 01743 709661

Extensive remains of 12th-century Cistercian Abbey.

IN AND AROUND IRONBRIDGE

(There is a family 'passport ticket' available for all the Ironbridge Gorge Museums. It is valid for a year, and can be used as often as required.)

Visitor Information Centre

The tollhouse at the Iron Bridge
☎ 01952 884391

The Iron Bridge

The world's first iron bridge, constructed by Abraham Darby III. Pedestrians and cyclists only.

Museum of Iron

At Coalbrookdale
Displays illustrating the history of iron and steel making in Coalbrookdale. Exhibits include Abraham Darby I's blast furnace.

Ironmasters' Homes

At Coalbrookdale
Houses of the Darby family, with records and artefacts.

Severn Warehouse Visitor Centre

Explains the development of industry in the Ironbridge Gorge. Audio-visual displays.

River Severn, Bridgnorth Low Town

Places to Visit

Blists Hill Open-Air Museum

50-acre-site with many reconstructed buildings and industrial workings, including the Hay Inclined Plane. Main feature is a re-creation of a Victorian town, with activities for children.

Enginuity

At Coalbrookdale
Interactive displays for young people, illustrating principles of science and engineering.

Coalport China Works Museum

This is the original factory of famous china manufacturers. It is now a museum.showing production methods with a comprehensive display of Coalport and Caughley china.

Jackfield Works and Tile Museum

Displays of decorative floor and wall tiles manufactured here from late 19th century to the 1960s.

Broseley Pipe Works

Across the river in Broseley
Clay pipe factory left as it was when it closed.

The Tar Tunnel

400yds (366m) tunnel, surviving from eighteenth-century bitumen mine.

Other attractions

Buildwas Abbey (English Heritage)

Off B4380, 1m (1km) west of Iron-bridge
Ruins dating from 1135, with substantial remains of church and notable chapter house.

Benthall Hall, Broseley (National Trust)

☎ 01952 882159
House basically of 16th century with noted plasterwork and panelling. Interesting church nearby.

IN AND AROUND MUCH WENLOCK

Visitor information

The Square.
☎ 01952 727679

The Priory

Ruins of notable 12th-century priory. Includes some famous carving.

The Guildhall

Finely preserved building of 1577 with open ground floor and upper chamber with superb woodwork.

Much Wenlock Museum

Memorial Hall, High Street
☎ 01952 727773
Well-designed displays illustrating geology, natural history and social history of the area.

Wenlock Pottery

Shineton Street

☎ 01952 727600

Working pottery with showroom.

Wenlock Edge

Famous limestone ridge to the NW of the town with fine views.

Shipton Hall

At Shipton, 7m (1) SW of Much Wenlock
Elizabethan house modified in 18th century. Original panelling and later plasterwork. Fine Georgian stable block and medieval dovecote. Privately owned but open to the public. Adjacent church is of interest.

IN AND AROUND BRIDGNORTH

Visitor Information

Listley Street

☎ 01746 763257

Guided walks

☎ 01746 767147 for information.

The Castle

At the end of East Castle Street
The site of the castle, behind St Mary's Church, is now a small park containing the remains of the keep, leaning at a startling angle.

Bishop Percy's House

In the Cartway
Fine example of a substantial three-storied timber-framed house.

The Wharf

Landscaped area, once the site of important river port. Backed by sandstone cliffs with caves once used for storage and habitation.

Cable Railway

Castle Terrace
The only inland cable railway in Britain, and the steepest. Drops 200ft (61m) down a cliff between High Town and Low Town.

Severn Valley Railway

☎ 01299 403816

Largest standard gauge preserved railway in Britain, running from Bridgnorth to Kidderminster. Bridgnorth station has the locomotive depot. Shop and refreshments.

Northgate Museum

☎ 01746 762830

History of the town and its people.

Dudmaston Hall (National Trust)

At Quatt, 3m (5km) S of Bridgnorth on A442

☎ 01746 780866

Late 17th-century house, with notable furniture and pictures, including 17th-century flower paintings and modern pictures. Shop, refreshments.

Rays Farm Country Matters

At Billingsley, on B4363, 8 miles (13km) S of Bridgnorth.

☎ 01299 841255

Extensive farm and wildlife park, with ancillary attractions.

To Kidderminster

It is best to take the main road (A442), which is pleasant enough with its wealth of roadside woodland and frequent cuttings through the prevailing sandstone.

Three miles (5 km) outside Bridgnorth, shortly after the village of Quatford, there is a chance to visit an outstanding National Trust property. **Dudmaston Hall** is a splendid Georgian house, containing a notable art collection and surrounded by attractive grounds. Two miles further on, **Hampton Loade** is a slightly ramshackle settlement very popular with fishermen, where there is space to park beside the river and inspect the primitive cable mechanism of the

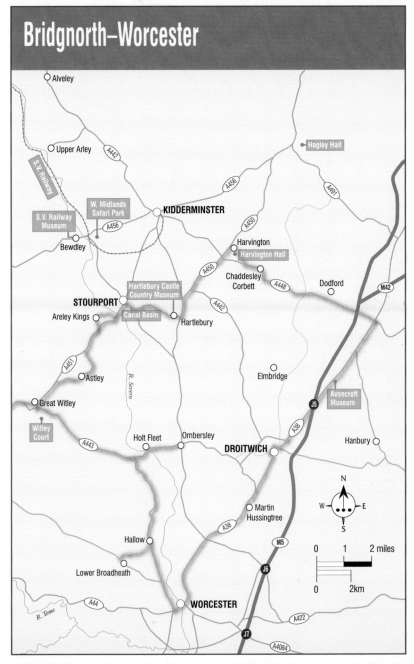

Bridgnorth–Worcester

Alveley

Upper Arley

A442

S.V. Railway

Hagley Hall

A456

A461

S.V. Railway
Museum

W. Midlands
Safari Park

KIDDERMINSTER

A450

A456

Bewdley

Harvington

Harvington Hall

M42

A450

Chaddesley
Corbett

Dodford

A448

Hartlebury Castle
Country Museum

STOURPORT

Areley Kings

Canal Basin

Hartlebury

A442

Astley

A451

R. Severn

Elmbridge

Great Witley

Avoncroft
Museum

J5

A38

Witley
Court

A443

Holt Fleet

Ombersley

DROITWICH

Hanbury

Martin
Hussingtree

Hallow

A38

M5

Lower Broadheath

J6

N
W E
S

0   1   2 miles

0   2km

R. Teme

A44

WORCESTER

A422

J7

A4084

passenger ferry. As you pass through the main road village of **Alveley** you may be surprised to see a substantial working-men's club in what seems to be a very rural spot. The club is the only reminder now that Alveley was once an outpost of a colliery that was centred at Highley on the other side of the river. Four miles (6km) before Kidderminster, a right turn takes you into **Upper Arley**, a very pleasant riverside village with a church, one or two pubs, a folly in the form of a fake medieval tower and a restored station on the Severn Valley Railway line that tends to feature in period films. On the approach to Kidderminster, the road swoops up and down dramatically, and the first sign of the town is a small and awkward roundabout at which some care is needed. Go straight on and follow the signs to the town centre.

Kidderminster is not noted for its tourist potential, and by comparison with its neighbours Bewdley and Stourport it is an unattractive town. Its reputation, of course, is based on carpet manufacture, but its 'milltown' character hides the fact that it was a very important textile centre from the thirteenth century onwards. The River Stour proved ideal for the fulling process, and Kidderminster achieved a reputation for cloth of great sophistication. It was not until the mid-eighteenth century that the first carpet loom was set up, and from that point the town began to take on the typical appearance of the Industrial Revolution, with functional mill buildings, huddled housing and numerous Nonconformist chapels.

Nowadays a town centre of this kind would be jealously guarded by a civic society anxious to preserve its distinctive atmosphere, but there was apparently no one to protest in the 1960s when much of the old town was flattened to accommodate a ruthless ring road and a gloomy pedestrian shopping precinct. The new road has isolated **St Mary's Church**, which stands on a hill with the canal passing below it, and attempts to beautify the site serve only to accentuate the ugliness around it. It is worth visiting the church, however, to see the way in which it reflects the confident prosperity of the town in its heyday; there are some notable early memorials in the rich Victorian interior.

The view from outside the church includes several impressive factory buildings, and enthusiasts for industrial archaeology will want to explore what remains of the close-knit mill quarter. It is still possible to walk through streets that are more reminiscent of Lancashire than Worcestershire. But most visitors will find little to detain them, and more attractive surroundings can quickly be reached by taking the Bewdley road (A456). There has been almost continuous housing development throughout this short distance, and the intervening village of Wribbenhall is now noticeable only as the site of the **West Midland Safari Park**, which occupies a former mansion and estate called Spring Grove. **Bewdley** is approached down a hill that has landed more than one vehicle in the river, and care is also needed to negotiate the sharp bend onto the bridge. To reach the car park drive into the main street and round behind the church.

Bewdley

The story usually told about Bewdley is that it was a flourishing town that went into sudden decline after its refusal to become the Severn junction of James Brindley's Worcestershire and Staffordshire canal (the town authorities are supposed to have dismissed the new waterway as a 'stinking ditch'). In fact the decision about the course of the canal was made on more considered grounds, but the result was certainly a transfer of economic dominance to neighbouring Stourport.

The prosperity of Bewdley came early. The nearby Tickenhill Manor was a royal palace under the Mortimers and for a time was the administrative centre of the Council of the Marches of Wales. A market was licensed early in the fifteenth century and borough status was achieved in 1472. In later years the town developed as a leading river port. Goods coming up the Severn from Bristol were distributed from here throughout the Midlands, and in the seventeenth and eighteenth centuries this privileged position gave Bewdley's own industries – mainly brass, horn and leather products – a considerable trading advantage.

A walk around Bewdley

The importance of the river in Bewdley's history is clearly seen from the bridge, designed by Thomas Telford and built in 1798. The older part of the town consists simply of a long waterfront with a compact commercial centre halfway along it. Load Street is more like a market square, closed off at one end by the church and at the other by the bridge. Nowadays this causes problems because the much-used bridge pours traffic straight into the town centre and forces it to squeeze painfully out at the other end.

The **waterfront** is undoubtedly the finest in the Midlands – a harmonious line of houses and shops in a variety of styles spanning several centuries. **Severnside South**, as it is rather unimaginatively called, has the grand buildings (those at the further end are particularly fine) but the short terrace to the north of the bridge is very attractive in its own way and reminiscent of a fishing village, although it was once a coal wharf. The hire boats along here, incidentally, are now moored to the redundant ferry that used to ply at Upper Arley, north of Kidderminster.

Load Street has a pleasing blend of Georgian and Victorian architecture with the occasional timber-framed house. Halfway up on the left-hand side is the sandstone **Guildhall** of 1808 with the old butchers' market, the **Shambles**, occupying a cobbled lane behind it. The market was purpose-built in 1783 with two arcades to accommodate the stalls, and a few years later three gaol cells were added at the far end. In 1971 the Bewdley Musuem Trust designed a conversion, and it now houses

Bewdley Station

displays illustrating the old industries of Bewdley and the Wyre Forest, local agricultural methods and the history of the town itself. There is space also for present-day craftsmen to demonstrate their skills. More recently an old **brass foundry** next door has been reconstructed to explain the history and techniques of the industry with occasional practical demonstrations. Other notable buildings in Load Street are the George Hotel, a former coaching inn almost opposite the Guildhall, and the half-timbered Bewdley Institute, which was also an inn until 1877.

St Anne's Church stands on an island amidst the traffic. Its seventeenth-century tower and eighteenth-century nave and chancel give it a curious hybrid appearance from the outside, but inside it is spacious and elegantly proportioned. There are few outstand-ing individual features, apart from the unusual pastel-tinted glass of its main windows. Behind the church Park Lane leads away uphill to **Tickenhill Manor**, eighteenth-century in style but containing traces of the earlier building that had royal associations. It has a niche in history as the scene of the marriage by proxy of Prince Arthur, Henry VIII's elder brother, to Catherine of Aragon in 1499. Back at the bottom of Park Lane a right turn brings you into **High Street**, where several buildings catch the eye. Almost immediately on the right is the richly timbered Bailiff's House of 1610 , while the Manor House, a little further along, is of roughly the same date.

The continuation of the High Street across the top of Lax Lane is called Lower Park and contains the early seventeenth-century **Sayers Almshouses** and a **Friends' Meeting House** of

1690, where the wife of Abraham Darby I is buried. Lower Park House was the birthplace of Stanley Baldwin, MP for Bewdley and Prime Minister during the Abdication crisis. The pleasant **Lax Lane** (thus called after the Danish word for salmon) runs down to the riverside and the distinguished range of buildings lining Severnside South.

While Bewdley has been content to grow old gracefully and without ambition, its neighbour **Stourport** has expanded aggressively, and it is difficult now to detect any break between the two towns. Stourport is reached by returning over the bridge and taking the minor road on the right almost immediately afterwards. A drive through ribbon development ends in a one-way system, and it is best to follow the signs for the riverside car parks where there is ample space for visitors.

Stourport

Stourport is one of the few English towns created entirely as a result of canal engineering, and the fact that the canal era coincided with a period of fine architecture ensured that the town's original nucleus is a very attractive place. When Brindley was seeking an outlet for his Worcestershire and Staffordshire Canal in the 1770s the obvious choice was the established port of Bewdley, but having considered the comparative engineering difficulties he set about building a port entirely from scratch at the hamlet of Mitton, 4m (6km) downstream. The central feature was a complex of basins and wharves, with warehouses, cottages and a large inn, all built in homogeneous style. The decline of the river and canal area brought a temporary desolation to the area, but luckily very little was lost, and in recent years Stourport has once again become a flourishing waterside community through the development of recreational boating.

A walk around Stourport

Nowadays Stourport is a favourite resort for Midlanders, and among the attractions for the day visitor are steamer trips and a funfair, so anyone who prefers quiet exploration should avoid bank holidays and summer weekends. On other days in the holiday season there is just the right level of boating activity to add vitality and interest to a walk through the old **canal terminal**, which is situated to the east of the fine iron road bridge of 1870.

Walk beneath the bridge (note the unusual spiral staircase) and along the path that leads past the funfair. A hump-backed bridge crosses the end of the lock, allowing access for narrow boats from the river to the first basin. The roofed section just beyond the lock is a dry dock. The path continues to the barge lock, designed for the much larger trows that were hauled in here from the river for unloading. The large brick building ahead is the famous **Tontine Hotel**, erected in the 1770s as a facility for merchants and boat-owners. Walk round the right-hand side of the Tontine and into **Mart Lane**. It runs up the side of the upper basin and provides an excellent view of the wide variety of craft moored here against a background of one of the original dock buildings (now the Stourport Yacht Club) surmounted by an elegant clock tower. Towards the top of Mart Lane are some merchants' houses, and Lichfield Street, the turning to the right at the top, also has examples of early dwellings.

The walk continues into **York Street**, reached by crossing Wallfield canal-bridge with its interesting tollhouse. This is one of Stourport's original streets and contains a pleasing blend of modest Georgian frontages. From the crossroads at the end it is possible to return to the river down busy **Bridge Street** or to extend the walk in the other direction into the High Street. This shopping centre marks the transition between the old town and the later development to the north, and although many of the buildings have been adapted to modern commercial use there are still some good Georgian facades on the eastern side. A right turn at the top of the High Street leads past the **Black Star**, a canal-side inn, and another right turn into Lion Hill leads back to the Wallfield Bridge.

Alternative Routes

1. via Witley Court to Worcester

The main road (A449) from Stourport to Worcester is fast and convenient but lacking in interest for the visitor who wants to explore this north Worcestershire countryside. Two alternative routes to Worcester are suggested here.

The first route begins on the A451. Cross Stourport bridge and almost at once look out for a right turn signposted Areley Kings Church. The village of **Areley Kings** is now something of a commuter dormitory, but the church and its associated buildings have been left in isolated tranquillity on the top of a hill overlooking the Severn valley. Architecturally the church is undistinguished inside or out, but it has a remarkable connection with

Layamon, author of the early English poem *Brut*, written in about 1200. The poet's introduction to his work indicates that he was parish priest here, and the fact was confirmed in 1886 when restoration work unearthed the base of a font inscribed with his name. The font can now be seen in the church. The churchyard is notable not only for a fine view but for the buildings on its perimeter.

The half-timbered Church House probably dates from the sixteenth century, and features something to be envied by every married man – a capacious garden house, built by the Revd Richard Vernon in 1728 as 'a retreat from domestic cares'. One final curiosity is the 'Coningsby Wall', a block of stone at the western edge of the churchyard. It was apparently inserted into the boundary wall of the churchyard at the behest of Sir Harry Coningsby, a member of the famous Herefordshire family, who retired here after accidentally drowning his son. Intended as his own memorial, it bears the inscription 'Lithologema quare: Reponitur Sir Harry', an eccentric trilingual declaration meaning 'Why a stone monument? Sir Harry lies here'. He died in 1701 and the block was later moved closer to his tomb.

As you leave this pleasant place and continue towards Great Witley it is worth making a brief diversion to **Astley**, reached by a turning to the left about 3m (5km) from Areley. Astley Hall was the home in later life of Prime Minister Stanley Baldwin, but less well known is Andrew Yarranton, who was born at nearby Yarhampton in 1616. He was a pioneer in industry and agriculture well before the more famous innovators of the eighteenth century. He is credited with the introduction of clover and sainfoin into the Midlands and was also a canal fanatic, carrying out navigational improvements between Stourbridge and Kidderminster. A few years ago one of his experimental iron furnaces was excavated by the river bridge between Yarhampton and Astley.

Less than a mile south of Astley is **Glasshampton monastery**, founded as an Anglican community in 1918 and housed in the stable block of a mansion that was later destroyed by fire. The original founder, Fr William Sirr, failed to establish his order, although a good many social outcasts found refuge there, but the buildings were taken over in 1947 by the Society of St Francis. The monastery is reached by a public track at the bridge that carries the B4196 over the river.

Back on the A451 you pass beneath Abberley Hill to reach **Great Witley**. It is an indeterminate sort of village, and to find its big attraction it is necessary to leave again on the A443, and watch out after nearly a mile for a turning on the right, signposted **Witley Court**. It leads to the most extraordinary ruin in the Midlands.

The A443 continues east and reaches the Severn at **Holt**. Holt actually consists of three settlements. The old village is downstream from the bridge and well off the main roads, while Holt Heath is a modern development on the A4133. Holt Fleet is a curious collection of dwellings, some permanent, some distinctly temporary and ramshackle, clustered round the bridge (yet another by Telford). It grew up in a random

Witley Court and Church

The original mansion acquired by Thomas Foley, son of a wealthy ironmaster in the late seventeenth century, from Stourbridge. The family were ambitious to become landed gentry, a process that was accelerated in 1712 when Foley's grandson became a Baron. He devoted much of his life to extending the house, and his widow had the parish church rebuilt in 1735, attaching it to one end of the mansion and thus making it something of a private chapel. The last of the Foleys added an enormous portico before the estate was sold to the future Earl of Dudley in 1838. He too added his share of extensions. The end result was a vast, sprawling residence conforming to no known architectural style. When it was seriously damaged by fire in 1937 it was left to disintegrate during the war, and only recently has a determined effort been made to save what is left. Under the direction of English Heritage the ruins of the house have been made safe, and, together with the extensive parkland, have been opened to visitors.

'Stunning' is the only word to describe the adjacent church. The plain exterior does not prepare you for the magnificence within. Amid a riot of gilt moulding 23 paintings decorate the ceiling, while ten windows by the same Venetian artist add further colour. A balustraded gallery at the west-end contains a very elegant organ, and the pulpit and lectern, though Victorian, match the rest of the exuberant decor. The dominant feature, however, is the huge monument to the first Lord Foley, a splendidly ostentatious piece of work. It is rather deflating to learn that this magnificent baroque interior was not lovingly created by the *nouveau riche* landowner; the ceiling paintings, windows and various other fittings were bought as a job lot when the Duke of Chandos sold his Edgware mansion in 1735.

Hartlebury Museum

Harvington Hall

sort of way to cater for river pursuits – fishing, sailing and boating – on this very attractive stretch of the Severn. It is a good place for a riverside walk, although it is difficult to leave the car without patronising the pub.

Rather than take the direct road to Worcester from here, cross the bridge and travel the two miles or so to **Ombersley**. Before it was bypassed, this attractive village used to be strangled by traffic, but now it is a pleasant experience to walk along the tranquil village street and look at some fine old houses. Several are timber-framed (the King's Arms is particularly impressive) but the brick cottages, especially the row opposite the church gate, contribute a good deal to the village's unpretentious charm. Ombersley is the domain of the Sandys family of nearby Ombersley Court, and their memorials are contained in a preserved section of the old church adjacent to the present St Andrew's, which looks richly medieval but is in fact an early example of nineteenth-century Gothic by Thomas Rickman. Like much of Rickman's work it has some fanciful features – the chancel, for example, is flanked by arches of almost oriental character embellished with icing-sugar decoration.

The final approach to Worcester entails a return to the A443. Three miles south of Holt Heath is Thorngrove House, home for a time of Lucien Bonaparte, Napoleon's brother, who was forced into exile for marrying an unsuitable wife. Almost immediately after come the first signs of Worcester's suburban sprawl, which has virtually destroyed the village character of Hallow. The big Victorian church is worth a visit, but before you reach it there is a chance to take the road to **Lower Broadheath** to see Elgar's birthplace (museum open to the public). The right turn is signposted in the middle of Hallow. The small cottage, close to the River Teme and facing the Malvern Hills, houses a large collection of scores and memorabilia relating to the life and work of the composer, and visitors have no difficulty in understanding why Elgar never lost his sense of belonging to this part of Worcestershire.

From here you enter **Worcester** on the west side of the river, and it is advisable to cross the bridge and seek out one of the riverside car parks rather than get involved in the city's complex traffic system.

2. Worcester via Harvington Hall and Droitwich

This involves leaving Stourport on the B4193, and the first feature of interest, **Hartlebury Castle**, comes after about 3m (5km). Bishops of Worcester lived here from the thirteenth century, although the original castle was virtually gutted during the Civil War. The present building is a dignified country house of predominantly eighteenth-century Gothic appearance, and is largely given over to the **Worcestershire County Museum**. The outstanding rooms of the Bishop's residence are the Great Hall, the Library and the Saloon, while the museum covers a vast range of interests relating to Worcestershire life and work.

The road now joins the A449 and it is necessary to turn left towards Kidderminster and then right onto the A450 after a mile (1km). Follow this road for another 2m (3km) to its junction with the A448 and turn right towards Bromsgrove. Very soon you arrive at **Harvington Hall** (open to the public), an Elizabethan moated manor house with rare wall paintings and a remarkable number of priest holes. Three miles (5km) later **Chaddesley Corbett** lies just off the road. This is a most attractive village with a main street of picture-postcard quality. The timber-framed Talbot Inn catches the eye, but the whole village deserves a leisurely walk. The church has a unique dedication to St Cassian and possesses a fine chancel and east window, but is noted mainly for a carved twelfth-century font.

About 3m (5km) further along the A448 it is worth turning off for **Dodford** to see the Edwardian church, a fascinating example of 'arts and crafts' building in an art nouveau style with decorations by the Bromsgrove Guild of craftsmen. The structure of the building, with its cloisters and outdoor pulpit, is unusual and its rose window is famous. The village, too, is of some interest since it was first laid out in 1848 as one of the Chartist 'National Land Scheme' projects.

If you now go into Bromsgrove and take the A38 (Worcester) road you will have the opportunity to visit the famous **Avoncroft Museum of Historic Buildings** at the southern edge of the town. Avoncroft is a fascinating museum of historic buildings spanning seven centuries, rescued and rebuilt on an open-air site. Apart from more conventional exhibits there is a 'tin chapel', a Victorian cell block and a 1940s prefab. From here it is a short run into **Droitwich**.

Droitwich

This is a town that makes no claim to beauty but has an unusually interesting history. The Romans had a small settlement here producing salt, and it was the salt of the Salwarpe valley that gave the town its medieval status – it gained a borough charter as early as the twelfth century. Salt is extracted from brine, and the early method of production was to use the brine that sprang naturally from the ground, but in the early eighteenth century pumps were introduced to force up purer and more concentrated brine. This led to the formation of subterranean caverns which have been a cause of subsidence ever since in the old part of the town.

It was no accident that as salt production diminished, Droitwich found new prosperity as a spa. During the spa craze people needed very little convincing that bathing in brine was beneficial, and in 1836 the Royal Baths were opened. Until recently modern treatment rooms were in operation, relying not so much on the curative powers of the brine as on its ability to support patients who could benefit from exercise in water. Now Droitwich's period as a spa has come to an end, but it has once again been offered a new lease of life as an overspill town with light industry.

The main interest for the visitor to Droitwich lies in the old town centre. The High Street certainly has a curiosity value with so many of its shops leaning at drunken angles because of subsidence. At the southern end of the street the old Town Hall retains its black and white elegance, with pilasters, cornices and striking windows, and in Friar Street beyond there are some pleasant

Georgian houses also sagging in unexpected places. Priory House graces the far end of Friar Street, although its effect is diminished by its position beneath an embankment carrying a new road.

St Andrew's Street, leading uphill from the Town Hall, contains the rambling length of the Raven Hotel, an odd mixture of genuine and reproduction timber-framing. It looks on to the newly developed Victoria Square with its modern shopping parades, one of which is in a remarkable mock Tudor style. Close by, in Heritage Way, is the **Droitwich Heritage Centre**, with displays illustrating the history and development of the town.

In 1197 Richard Wych was born in Droitwich. He entered the church and made rapid progress, becoming Chancellor of Oxford University and Bishop of Chichester. After his death he was canonised as St Richard of Chichester and is commemorated in an astonishing mosaic in the Roman Catholic church in Worcester Road. The town's two medieval parish churches, St Andrew's and St Peter's, are also worth visiting, but can boast nothing as striking.

The most impressive building here is about half a mile to the north off the A38. The dominant figure in the more recent history of Droitwich was John Corbett, the nineteenth-century industrialist who centralised salt production at Stoke Prior to the north-east of the town and played a major part in the development of the spa. In 1869 he commissioned a French architect to build him a mansion near the town (he allegedly wanted to give his French wife something to remind her of home). The result was a huge and highly embellished house in the style of a Loire chateau; in fact it has always been known as **Chateau Impney**.

From Droitwich the main A38 road to Worcester passes through **Martin Hussingtree**, which has some picturesque buildings, including the handsome eighteenth-century rectory and Court Farm of a century earlier. The churchyard is the resting place of Thomas Tomkins, organist at Worcester Cathedral for 53 years, whose status as a composer might have been greater if he had not been forced into retirement by the Puritan regime. He lived at Court Farm during the last years of his life. If you are not familiar with Worcester, which has a reputation for being hostile to strange motorists, it is advisable to follow the A38 into the city and turn right just before the centre to park by the riverside.

Ombersley

Chaddesley Corbett

Places to Visit

IN AND AROUND KIDDERMINSTER

Severn Valley Railway

☎ 01299 403816

Southern terminus adjacent to mainline station.

Bodenham Arboretum and Earth Centre

4m (6km) N of Kidderminster off A442

☎ 01562 852444

Rare trees and plants, in landscaped parkland with lakes. Restaurant and gift shop.

Arley Arboretum

6m (10km) NW of Kidderminster off A442

☎ 01299 861368

Fine specimen trees in park overlooking Severn valley.

Stone House Cottage Gardens

2m (3km) SE of Kidderminster on A448

☎ 01562 69902

Walled gardens with over 3,000 plants. Nursery sales.

Hartlebury Castle

Official residence of the Bishops of Worcester. Staterooms include medieval Great Hall remodelled in seventeenth century, eighteenth-century library.

Hereford and Worcester County Museum

Hartlebury Castle, 4m (6km) S of Kidderminster off A449

☎ 01299 250416

Very wide-ranging displays relating to natural history, archaeology, trades, industries, social history, etc.

Harvington Hall

3m (5km) SE of Kidderminster

☎ 01562 777846

Tudor moated-manor house, with wall paintings, priest holes and Georgian chapel. Gift shop and restaurant.

Hagley Hall

7m (12km) NE of Kidderminster, off A456.

☎ 01562 882408

Magnificent mid-eighteenth-century house, fine furniture and paintings. 350-acre (865hec) landscaped park.

IN AND AROUND BEWDLEY AND STOURPORT

Visitor Information

Load Street, Bewdley

☎ 01299 404740

Bewdley Museum

Load Street

☎ 01299 403573

In the former Shambles, the museum is devoted mainly to local life and history, in particular the trades and industries of the district. Includes a working brass foundry and modern craftsmen's shops.

Severn Valley Railway

Bewdley Station
☎ 01299 403816
Frequent steam trains in summer, also model railway display, shop and refreshments.

Wyre Forest Visitor Centre

3m (5km) SW of Bewdley on A456
☎ 01299 266944
Woodland trails, cycling routes, restaurant.

West Midlands Safari and Leisure Park

☎ 01299 402114
On the A456 between Bewdley and Stourport. Drive-round tours of impressive animal reserves and wide variety of amusements.

Stourport Canal Basins

Junction of the Staffordshire and Worcestershire Canal, constructed by James Brindley in the late 18th century. Much of the complex survives and is in use for pleasure craft. Original buildings include Tontine Hotel and range of offices and warehouses.

Witley Court (English Heritage)

On A443, 6m (10km) SW of Stourport
☎ 01299 896636
Ruins of spectacular mansion, with gardens and woodland walks. Adjacent is magnificent baroque church of St Peter.

IN AND AROUND DROITWICH

Heritage Centre

St Richard's House, Victoria Square
☎ 01905 774312
Local history, especially of salt industry and spa. Temporary exhibitions. Also Visitor Information Centre.

Church of the Sacred Heart

Worcester Road
Superb mosaic decorations commemorating St Richard of Chichester.

Avoncroft Museum of Buildings

At Stoke Heath, 4½ m (7½km) NE of Droitwich
☎ 01527 831363
Unique collection of restored and re-erected buildings, including windmill, granary, chain-making workshop, timber-framed houses, post-war prefabricated buildings.

Hanbury Hall (National Trust)

4m (6½km) E of Droitwich
☎ 01527 821214
House of 1701, with fine furniture and porcelain. Outstanding feature is series of painted ceilings.

Jinny Ring Craft Centre

At Hanbury, 4m (6½km) NE of Droitwich
☎ 01527 821272
Workshops for weaving, pottery, glass, woodcarving, etc. Shop and restaurant.

Chateau Impney

1m (1½km) N of Droitwich off A38
Flamboyant 19th-century hotel, originally a mansion built in French chateau style.

3. Worcester and the Malverns

Worcester

Worcester may well be one of the oldest settlements in England, having been continuously occupied since the fifth century. A camp was established here by the Romans even earlier, and when civilian occupation started after the Roman withdrawal there is evidence that iron was an important product here, with ore probably being boated up from the Forest of Dean. Later the town became a local Anglo-Saxon capital, and in 680 the first cathedral was built. After the Norman invasion Bishop Wulfstan co-operated with the invaders, ensuring that he was the only Anglo-Saxon bishop to retain his diocese.

Opposite page & left:
The Guildhall, Worcester

Worcester and the Malverns

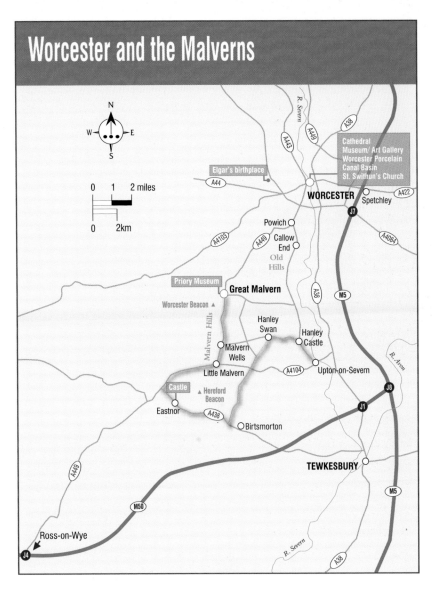

N W E S

0 1 2 miles

0 2km

Elgar's birthplace

Cathedral
Museum/ Art Gallery
Worcester Porcelain
Canal Basin
St. Swithun's Church

A44

WORCESTER

Spetchley

A422

J7

Powich

Callow
End

Old
Hills

A449

A4103

A4084

M5

A38

Priory Museum

Great Malvern

Worcester Beacon ▲

Malvern Hills

Hanley
Swan

Hanley
Castle

Malvern
Wells

Little Malvern

A4104

Upton-on-Severn

R. Avon

Castle

▲ Hereford
Beacon

J8

Eastnor

A438

J1

Birtsmorton

TEWKESBURY

A449

M50

M5

Ross-on-Wye

J4

R. Severn

A38

Medieval Worcester was a centre of the cloth-making industry, but the decline of the craft in the sixteenth century left the city greatly impoverished, a situation that was not improved when Worcester took the Royalist side in the Civil War. Its loyalty to the King gave it its title 'The Faithful City', but when the decisive battle of war was fought outside the city and won by Cromwell the inhabitants received harsh treatment.

Recovery began with the development of the glove industry, a product for which Worcester was famous well into the twentieth century, and was helped by Worcester's increasing importance as a market town, an administrative centre and a focus of social life. From the late eighteenth century onwards it prospered as a commercial and manufacturing centre, becoming world-famous for at least two of its products – Royal Worcester china and Worcestershire Sauce. The city's commercial history was greatly assisted by its position on the Severn, which gave it access to important trading centres like Gloucester and Bristol.

The development of modern Worcester has been the subject of heated debate ever since the 1950s, when plans were first put forward for the reshaping of the city centre. At that time the city was a very picturesque place. It had a long waterfront of residential and commercial buildings to the north and south of the bridge. The area around the cathedral and behind the main street abounded in old cottages and shops, threaded by narrow lanes.

During the 1960s a massive clearance took place. For years a major problem was traffic congestion caused by the solitary bridge feeding traffic into narrow streets, and this has led to new roads being given disproportionate priority within the city. A second bridge has now been constructed to the south, but it is well outside the city boundary and seems to have done little to alleviate the problem except at peak commuter periods.

In recent years much has been done to improve the river frontage to the north of the bridge, but to the south there remains an undistinguished riverside scene. The area in front of the cathedral consists mainly of a large roundabout and associated roads, and there are only occasional reminders of Worcester's medieval heritage.

All this is mentioned, not to revive old controversies, but to warn the visitor not to expect too much. Much picturesque townscape has been lost, but enough remains to make a stroll around the city rewarding.

A walk around Worcester

The best place to start is on the **bridge**. There is a much-photographed view of the cathedral from here, and the sight of the warehouse-style flats is a reminder of the part the river has played in Worcester's history. For centuries there was a thriving trade with the port of Bristol, and the city's main importance as an inland port was enhanced with the arrival of the Worcester and Birmingham Canal in 1815. The main dock area was at Diglis, beyond the cathedral, but old photographs show the quayside between the cathedral and the bridge lined with small commercial craft. On the other side of the river is the county cricket ground, reckoned to be one of the most attractive in England.

Walk into the city by way of **Bridge Street**, which is unimpressive now but was designed at the same time as the bridge to afford a grand entrance into the town centre. Bear right into **Deansway**, a 1960s road constructed for the benefit of through traffic. The redevelopment resulted in All Saints' Church on your right being deprived of its parish and left high and dry on a raised bank. Medieval in origin, the church was rebuilt in 1740 in the restrained classical style characteristic of the period.

Deansway is an undistinguished street, but overshadowing it is the soaring **'Glover's Needle'**, a superbly graceful spire in a commanding situation. It is all that is left of St Andrew's Church, which was demolished in 1950. Fortunately a decision was made to retain the medieval tower, which had been adorned with its spire by Nathaniel Wilkinson in 1751, with no other motive, it seems, but local pride. The whole structure is 250ft (75m) high. At the top of Deansway on the right is the Old Palace, a mid-eighteenth-century house that was the Bishop's town residence until about 1840, when it was decided that he could manage with Hartlebury Castle. It was then used as the Deanery but today serves as a diocesan centre. Actually the Georgian facade conceals earlier structures of various dates, including a fourteenth-century basement known as the 'Abbot's Kitchen'.

At the end of Deansway the north side of the cathedral comes fully into view and so does the most dramatic result of redevelopment. As you face the roundabout, with your back to Deansway, the pedestrianised High Street leads away to the left, while the massive bulk of contemporary building in front is the Giffard Hotel with its associated shopping precinct. By way of contrast, some of the original character of this area can be seen around the corner to the right. This is Cathedral Yard, an oddly isolated survival comprising a handsome Georgian terrace with a raised pavement, hinting at what was once a quietly elegant cathedral close. Access to the cathedral is across the green and through the north door.

The cathedral close is College Green, originally the site of Worcester Castle and now a pleasant square lined with handsome buildings, many of them belonging to the King's School. At the river end the **Watergate** gives access to the riverbank, where marks on a wall indicate the extraordinary flood levels the Severn has reached in past years. At the other end of College Green the Edgar Tower, the castle gateway dating from the reign of King John, forms an impressive entrance from the city.

As you emerge from College Green through the Edgar Tower, Severn Street leads away to the right. This is the way to one of the city's most popular tourist attractions, the **Royal Worcester Porcelain** works.

Worcester porcelain was the result of scientific experiments by John Wall, a local man of many parts who was a physician at the Royal Infirmary, a populariser of the Malvern waters and a dabbler in applied chemistry. It was in 1751 that he set up a company

*Worcester Cathedral from the Edgar Tower and
(opposite) the Cathedral nave*

Worcester Cathedral

Although there were monastic foundations here well before the Normans, the earliest parts of the present building date from the reconstruction begun in 1084 by Bishop Wulfstan, the only Saxon bishop allowed to keep his diocese after the Norman invasion. After collapse in 1175 and a fire soon afterwards a long period of rebuilding began in 1218, and there was extensive restoration in the 1870s.

Detailed guides are available and only the more distinctive features of the cathedral can be mentioned here. The extreme west end is the oldest part of the nave (mid-twelfth century) although the large west window is by John Hardman and dates from the Victorian restoration. The nave was not finally completed until 1377. There are some fine tombs and monuments here, notably those of two former bishops – Thornborough and Hough – and the Worcester merchant Robert Wilde. More recent memorials include those to Stanley Baldwin, the novelist Francis Brett Young and Mrs Henry Wood, a Worcester lady famous as the author of *East Lynne*.

The choir is a most graceful structure with octagonal columns of sandstone and marble and a general effect of lightness. In the centre is the tomb of King John who, at his own request, was the first post-Conquest king to be buried in England. The tomb thus has the oldest royal effigy in England, constructed in fine Purbeck marble. On the south side of the choir is the elaborate tomb of Prince Arthur, eldest son of Henry VII, who died in 1502. His chantry was built two years later and much of its splendour survives in spite of Puritan vandalism. The choir stalls have a set of misericords heavily restored in the nineteenth century.

Two of the original features of the cathedral should not be missed. The crypt is a magnificent Norman structure, while the Chapter House, reached from the south aisle, is unusual in being round with a central column.

EDWARD ELGAR O. M.
MASTER OF THE KING'S MUSICK
1857 — 1934
PROFICISCERE ANIMA CHRISTIANA DE HOC MUNDO

with the aim of copying the Chinese porcelain so popular at the time. The modern company is a direct descendant of Wall's enterprise and continues to produce celebrated collectors' pieces. The complex now houses, in addition to the museum, a factory shop and facilities for children's activities.

After returning to the top of Severn Street, turn right into Sidbury, cross the road and walk the hundred yards or so to the canal bridge, where the unobtrusive Commandery entrance is signposted. **The Commandery** got its name because it was the headquarters of the Royalist army at the battle of Worcester in 1651, but in fact the building is much older, having served as a monastic hospital and lodging house from about 1465. A programme of restoration has ensured the survival of the impressive timber-framed structure, and it is now a branch of the museum service, specialising, appropriately, in Civil War exhibits. Refreshments can be taken on the canalside terrace.

Walk back up Sidbury and cross the junction with the City Walls Road. (Anyone interested in industrial archaeology may want to walk a short distance along City Walls Road to look at the former Fownes Gloves factory – a massive nineteenth-century rectangular block, now a hotel.) Take the next turning on the right into **Friar Street**, which contains some of the city's oldest buildings.

Immediately on the left is the Old Talbot Inn, a hostelry that has had many uses in its time: it was originally an ecclesiastical house connected with the cathedral and later became the meeting place of the City Magistrates. **Tudor House**, a little further along on the same side, is another outpost of the City Museum and a very entertaining one. Dating from the fifteenth century, the house has also had a variety of uses as an inn, a shop, a tearoom and a clinic, but since 1971 it has housed the museum's 'folk' exhibits charting the history of everyday life in the area.

Almost immediately opposite are the **Laslett Almshouses**, built around an attractive quadrangle and looking comparatively modern. In fact they were erected in 1912 to replace some rather unsatisfactory accommodation in the old prison. Next door is Worcester's finest timber-framed building, the **Greyfriars**. Of late fifteenth-century date, it was, despite its name, the house of a wealthy merchant, and was magnificently restored by private owners, although it now belongs to the National Trust. There is a most attractive garden behind.

Friar Street extends into **New Street** where there is also much of interest. To the left, the Market Hall has an interesting mid-Victorian frontage, while facing it is another fine timber-framed building, the three-storey **Nash's House**. John Nash helped to establish glove-making in the city in the sixteenth century, and among the benefactions of the family were the **Nash and Wyatt Almshouses** which, in their rebuilt form, can be seen by walking down Nash's Passage.

Finally, on the corner of New Street and the Cornmarket is another of Worcester's famous tourist attractions, **King Charles's House**. It has been restored to a suitably picturesque condition, although the two timber-framed

'Glover's Needle' between Deansway and the river

Opposite: King Charles II escaped from Worcester through this house in New Street

sections are separated by a brick addition built after a fire in the eighteenth century. The house achieved fame after the battle of Worcester when Charles II, pursued by his Parliamentarian enemies, made his escape through the back door which opened onto the other side of the city wall.

The **Cornmarket** used to be an intimate square until demolition for the new City Walls Road opened up one side, but it is still a pleasant oasis with attractive shops and a fine Victorian pub on one corner. Easily overlooked at the back of the pub is **Old St Martin's church**, externally undistinguished but with an interesting interior of the traditional Anglo-Catholic kind. **Mealcheapen Street**, one of the oldest in Worcester, leads out of the Cornmarket towards the city centre and passes through an ancient commercial district. Many of the buildings along here have been modernised – the opened-up courtyard of the Reindeer Inn is particularly successful – but it still retains more atmosphere than most of the neighbouring streets.

At the top of Mealcheapen Street is **St Swithun's church**, one of the best-preserved early eighteenth-century churches in Britain. It is now redundant, but its preservation has been secured, and rightly so because it is a gem, with its elegant proportions, restrained plasterwork, high box pews, gilded sanctuary columns and above all its splendid three-decker pulpit. The street behind it is the Trinity and contains Queen Elizabeth's House, so called because the Queen is reputed to have addressed the citizens from its balcony during her visit in 1575.

You now emerge at the Cross, still the hub of Worcester although the traffic that used to dominate it has been diminished by the pedestrianisation of High Street. Turning right towards the railway bridge over Foregate Street, the buildings reflect better than anything else the city's past commercial prosperity. On the east side there is a very handsome range comprising two banks, St Nicholas's Church and the old **Hopmarket Hotel**. The latter is an imposing Victorian structure, part of a complex that used to include warehouses and a market, and it has been imaginatively converted to accommodate small shops and craft establishments with flats above. Opposite is the Star, a former coaching inn much older than it looks.

The railway bridge marks the end of the shopping centre but it is worth walking further along Foregate Street to reach another impressive Victorian building that houses the **library, art gallery and museum**. Nineteenth-century work is a particular feature of the gallery's permanent collection, and there is usually a touring exhibition to see. The museum has some varied displays ranging from geology and natural history to a complete reconstruction of a traditional chemist's shop. The neoclassical **Shire Hall** of 1834 is set back from the road just beyond the museum, but the finest feature of Foregate Street is the long line of Georgian facades on the opposite side.

Walk back along the west side of Foregate Street and note the inconspicuous entrance to the **Berkeley Hospital** on the other side of the railway bridge. The Berkeley family, whose ancestral home is Berkeley Castle near Bristol, has strong connections with Worcester (King Charles's House was their town residence) and the present Hospital was built by Robert Berkeley in 1692 in a Dutch style. It is charmingly arranged around a flagged courtyard with a chapel at one end.

Almost opposite St Nicholas's Church the narrow Angel Street makes an interesting diversion. At the point where it joins Angel Place there is the refurbished **Corn Exchange** of 1848, a solid, confident building with a colonnaded front. Next to it the old Scala is another and older example of classic cinema architecture. Angel Place runs into Broad Street, and a left turn brings you to the former Crown Inn, once Worcester's handsomest coaching inn and now converted into a shopping arcade.

Return to the Cross and turn right into the High Street. Apart from the shops there is nothing of great interest until you reach the city's finest secular building, the **Guildhall**. This masterpiece of 1722 has a richly embellished facade that includes statues of Charles and Queen Anne and a caricature of Cromwell's head over the main door. The Guildhall is open to visitors and the great attraction is the assembly room on the first floor, with its beautifully embossed and painted ceiling, its chandeliers and a small stage enhanced with delicate columns. This room was the scene of countless 'routs' – those provincial dances that were an essential part of the social life of the country gentry.

You are now back in the area that has been progressively remodelled since the 1960s. The nearby Crown-gate shopping centre looks typical of its kind, but if you venture into it you will find the exquisite **Countess of Huntingdon's Church**, the subject of a campaign by John Betjeman when it was considered for demolition. It was built in 1804, though the Countess first visited Worcester to establish her version of Methodism in 1769. It now has a new function as the Huntingdon Hall, a venue for a varied programme of concerts and events.

On to the Malverns

The way out of Worcester is the A449 (for Malvern). The first village you reach is **Powick**, which has a significant place in history. The old Powick bridge, a venerable structure of fifteenth-century origin, was the scene of a very early skirmish in the Civil War. In September 1642 a consignment of valuable plate from various Oxford colleges was dispatched to Worcester as a contribution to the King's war funds. Pursuing Parliamentary forces made half-hearted attempt to enter the city but were repulsed, and having retired to Powick they were attacked by Royalist cavalry under Prince Rupert. After a bloody but indecisive engagement the Parliamentarians lost heart and retreated.

It was a different story in 1651 when Cromwell was triumphant in the decisive battle of the Civil War, fought mainly in the nearby fields on the far side of the new Powick bridge. Details of the battle are remembered by historians only; what has passed into folklore is Charles's escape afterwards and his much-delayed voyage to France.

Worcester has many fascinating shops waiting to tempt you!

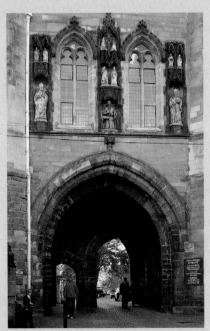

Edgar Tower

Royal Worcester

Above: The Commandery,
Sidbury, Worcester

Right: The Greyfriars,
Friar Street

Powick itself is a big and scattered settlement that has lost much of its character, although the church is worth visiting for a notable tomb of 1786 to a Mrs Russell by the artist Thomas Scheemakers. The village's most famous, or notorious, building was its Hospital, originally the County Lunatic Asylum, which had the distinction of employing the young Edward Elgar as the conductor of the inmates' band.

The hills now loom ever nearer and the outskirts of Malvern are reached at **Newland**, a village where the splendid Victorian church is in a French Gothic style and stands near a set of almshouses provided by the Beauchamp family, whose principal home is Madresfield Court, a mile away. Evelyn Waugh was a frequent guest here, and his novel *Brideshead Revisited* is thought to have been inspired by his visits.

The Malverns

The 9m (15km) range of the Malvern Hills rises sharply in an otherwise level landscape and presents a stark and distinctive silhouette. The hills look high but in fact they reach only 1,400ft (425m) at their two highest points, and it is their accessibility that accounts for their popularity throughout the Midlands. Despite Victorian encroachment on the slopes at Great Malvern itself, the hills have remained free of intrusive development, thanks to the Malvern Hills Conservators, an old-established body with effective powers. There has been a certain amount of quarrying for the extremely hard pre-Cambrian rock, but the old workings are now well screened; indeed they are now something of an asset because they make visible the strata of the underlying stone. Moreover, a good deal of the charm of the town is due to the use of this local building material. Some suggestions for exploring the hills are included later in the chapter.

Great Malvern

The town is the natural centre of the string of settlements along the hills. Leaving aside very early history, Malvern first acquired status as the site of a monastic foundation at the end of the eleventh century, although its situation well away from natural lines of communication discouraged the development of a town. At the Dissolution, Malvern was no more than a village, and it remained so until the turn of the eighteenth century, when its waters began to achieve fame for their curative properties. Dr John Wall (the moving spirit behind the Worcester Porcelain Company) first published an analysis of the waters as early as 1757. His novel claim was that their benefit derived from their purity and not from any mineral content, and this reputation still supports the thriving sale of bottled Malvern water.

Like many other towns, Malvern went on to prosper from the spa cult of the nineteenth century, although it never became the sort of fashionable resort that acquired a dubious reputation. Indeed the hydropathic treatment at Malvern was not simply a matter of meeting to sip the waters but a spartan regime of cold douches and cold walks. This high-minded attitude is reflected in the architecture of the town, which has none of the expensive elegance of

Bath or Cheltenham, and certainly no frivolity. Instead there is a preponderance of solid Victorian villas, although it must be said that some of them show individual and sometimes adventurous taste, and their general effect has been to create a leafy spaciousness in the roads near the town centre.

A walk around Great Malvern

The best place to start a walk around the town is in **Belle Vue Terrace**, a short length of the A449 that cuts across the top of Malvern and forms its highest shopping street. The Terrace lives up to its name because from here the Priory and the other major buildings can be seen against a backdrop of much of the county of Worcestershire. At the height of the water-cure period this was the centre of activity. The Mount Pleasant Hotel at the southern end is the only surviving hotel of the time, while Lloyds Bank next door stands on the site of the first hydropathic centre of 1842. Next door again the shop was once the Belle Vue Hotel, and the building still retains much of its original appearance. Further along there are two other shops of interest: the impressive Pharmacy fulfilled this function for visitors in town for the cure, and WH Smith's was Malvern's Post Office in stagecoach days.

Just around the corner of the northern end of the Terrace is the **Unicorn Inn**, self-consciously quaint now, but with genuine timber-framing and one of Malvern's oldest survivals. Another interesting group stands on the opposite side of the road. Barclays Bank is in the best Grecian style of the Regency period and

was erected to house the Royal Library, with the 'Coburg Baths' incorporated into the other section of the building. These two establishments formed an important social centre, since the Library offered a range of cultural activities to complement the serious business of medical treatment. Equally typical of its period, the adjacent Foley Arms is a handsome coaching inn of 1810.

Immediately below Belle Vue Terrace is the open space that was once the 'village green' of medieval Malvern. Walk over to the south side and down the road leading to the **Abbey Gateway**, noting on the left the shop built in a well-meaning 'Gothic' style. The Gateway spans the road and looks impressively medieval, but its nineteenth-century reconstruction left little of the original work visible. The nearby Abbey Hotel looks much more venerable but dates from 1849. The backs of houses are always instructive, and a glance at the huge Victorian house up on the right reveals some remarkable architectural details in the timbering and windows.

Continue down Abbey Road and turn left into Grange Road, passing the site of the original priory, now covered by hotel buildings. On the right is the pleasant Priory Park and then the former Winter Gardens, now known as **Malvern Theatres**. The first buildings here were the Assembly Rooms, essential for a spa but appearing rather belatedly in 1884. In the 1920s the present building was erected to house a theatre and other amenities, and up to the Second World War it was the venue of the famous Malvern Festival where several of George Bernard Shaw's plays received their first performances.

Elgar looking at the former Bluebird Tea Rooms (below)

Malvern Water spring, The Belle Vue Terrace

Abbey Gatehouse, Museum

Walking on the Malvern Hills

The walk from the town centre to St Ann's Well has already been mentioned. There is insufficient space here to provide detailed walking routes, but these can be found on an excellent website, **www.countrywalkers.co.uk**, and also in leaflets available at the Visitors' Information Centre. The highest point on the Hills is the Worcestershire Beacon 1,394ft (425m) with North

Hill 1,307ft (397m) and the British Camp Hill Herefordshire Beacon 1,114ft (338m) the other

highest points. The entire length of the Hills is open to the public.

For short walks the best starting points are the car parks. The Wyche Cutting car park, on the B4218 from Malvern to Colwall, is the highest and the best for a climb to the Worcestershire Beacon. For the Herefordshire Beacon it is best to use the British Camp car park on the A449 Malvern to Ledbury road. There are also car parks at the extreme ends of the Hills – at the north is the Clock Tower park on North Malvern Road, and to the south the park at Hollybush on the A438.

For the less able there are 'easier access' paths leading from disabled parking spaces at Blackhill Car Park on Jubilee Drive (B4232 road from Wyche Cutting to British Camp on the western side of the Hills) and at Earnslaw Quarry on Wyche Road (B4218). There are public toilets at St Ann's Well, the Wyche Cutting and at British Camp.

A path immediately opposite the Winter Gardens leads round to the main door of the **Priory**, one of England's outstanding parish churches. It has had a chequered history. Begun in the eleventh century and still basically Norman, its present form is largely the result of extensive rebuilding between 1400 and 1460, yet only 79 years after this complete renewal it was surrendered to Henry VIII at the Dissolution. The other Priory buildings were very quickly disposed of to opportunist buyers and a start was made on demolishing the church. Then, at the last moment, the inhabitants of the tiny village offered to buy it from the King to replace their old church. They got it for £20, but the maintenance of the huge building was another matter; it proved such a burden that by the beginning of the nineteenth century the church was in a serious state of disrepair and hardly usable. Not until 1860 was radical restoration put in hand, so it is surprising that so much survives in a building of immense beauty.

There is an immediate impression of space upon entering because nothing impedes the view of the entire length of nave and chancel. As so often with Victorian restoration most attention was given to the east end, so there is a marked contrast between the solid strength of the nave and the lighter richness of the chancel. The nave arcades of six bays are supported by massive pillars, and some of the fifteenth-century granite can be seen towards the top. Although the tower divides the east and west ends there is very little sense of its presence thanks to the lofty arches beneath it.

The interior features of the Priory are described in great detail in a booklet illustrated in colour and available at the bookstall. There is a notable array of fifteenth-century glass, not only in the east window but in the clerestory, the north transept and the west window, while good Victorian glass can be seen in St Anne's Chapel (south choir aisle). The misericords are all in place in the monks' stalls in the choir, although the originals are mixed with nineteenth-century restorations or replicas – the carvings include ten of the twelve 'Labours of the Months'. The Priory's most famous possession, however, is a collection of well over a thousand medieval tiles, locally made. Some are incorporated into the altar screen but most are to be found in the north choir aisle. It is perhaps worth pointing out the ironic fact that the most elaborate tomb here, between the choir and St Anne's Chapel, commemorates John Knotsford, the Elizabethan entrepreneur mainly responsible for demolishing most of the other monastic buildings.

After leaving the Priory you can continue the tour of the town centre by walking back to the Winter Gardens and strolling through **Priory Park**. The gardens are small but cleverly landscaped and include several varieties of exotic trees and the Swan Pool, originally the monks' fish pond. Two very contrasting buildings can be seen by leaving at the north gate: Priory Park mansion is a remarkable example of unrestrained Victorian Gothic, while Portland House (on the opposite side of Church Street) is in severe classical style.

Malvern's real character is to be found by walking along some of the spacious roads lined with Victorian architecture in infinite variety. Highly recommended are Graham Road, which runs north from Church Street, and Avenue Road. The latter branches off almost opposite Portland House and leads to the interesting railway station, but for the architectural enthusiast the main attraction will probably be the huge facade of the **Girls' College**, designed by EW Elmslie as the Imperial Hotel in 1861.

The Malvern Hills

Victorian building development was strongly influenced by Viscountess Foley, who adopted the role of Lady of the Manor and imposed much of her own distinctive taste on the town (among other decrees she is reputed to have stipulated that none of the larger houses built in her time should be similar). Among her other achievements was the embellishment of **St Ann's Well**, one of Malvern's natural springs. It can be visited by returning to Belle Vue Terrace and taking the lane that starts at the Unicorn Inn. The Well is one point on a circular walk around the lower contours of the hills on a well-defined path that passes through Rushy Valley to the south and goes on to provide a fine view of the town, including the famous Malvern College. Soon after passing Earnslaw quarry and pool, and just short of the Wyche cutting, the track turns onto the other side of the ridge and proceeds northwards, taking in the former site of the Royal Well Spa and the indicator stone

on the north side of the Worcestershire Beacon. From here there is a zigzag progress back to St Ann's Well.

A walk along the ridge

Enthusiastic ramblers may well want to spend a day on the complete ridgetop walk (about 10m or 16km). It makes sense to start at the northern end where the climbing is steeper, and, after parking at the Clock Tower car park on North Malvern Road, there is a path up to North Hill. It is a steep ascent between disused quarries. Once on the top there are two summits visible ahead. Purists will no doubt want to walk over the Sugar Loaf before tackling the Worcestershire Beacon, but others may prefer to take the comfortable track around to the right.

Various paths lead to the top of the Beacon, which is so popular that a cafe operates on a seasonal basis (but do not rely on finding it open). A toposcope helps to identify the features of the view from the top. Some of the markings are a little optimistic but it is a splendid panorama, and the sense of height is such that it is easy to forget that you are standing at only 1,400ft (425m). A well-defined path leads off and down directly to the Wyche Cutting, where the B4218 crosses the hills.

The next length of ridge is pleasantly undulating and the path starts to run close to the Shire Ditch, a thirteenth-century boundary created by the Earl of Gloucester and the Bishop of Hereford to mark the division between their hunting grounds. Later it was part of the county boundary between Worcestershire and Herefordshire. Wynd's Point,

Below: Walking in
the Malvern Hills

Elgar's birthplace (above) Elgar Museum (below)

the end of this section, is a very popular spot for visitors seeking a short route to the Herefordshire Beacon, and it is also a convenient place for a refreshment break.

At 1,100ft (335m) the Beacon is another magnificent viewpoint, this time towards the rougher, less inhabited country to the west of the hills. It is also the site of an Iron Age hill fort with some spectacular ramparts and ditches. Comparatively few people venture further south, but this section, through a broken and wooded landscape, makes a pleasant change from the exposed ridge to the north.

The path continues to follow the Shire Ditch below Hangman's Hill, passing an outcrop containing the mysteriously named Clutter's Cave. The obelisk over on the right is in the grounds of Eastnor Castle and commemorates members of the Somers family. Several tracks meet at the point known as Silurian Pass (to mark an underlying bank of younger Silurian stone) and the way lies over or round the modest Swinyard Hill. The dangerous Gullet Quarry lies straight ahead and it is best to skirt it on the right before making for Midsummer Hill 930ft (285m). A track that skirts the hill on the right avoids the climb, but you can branch east to pass through the 'north gates' of the Iron Age ramparts. Inside the ramparts there are paths leading to Midsummer Hill or to Hollybush Hill, its neighbour to the east.

In fact the route by way of Hollybush Hill is possibly the more interesting, if longer, because the descent is through the 'south gates' of the fort, which have been extensively excavated, and then through the old Hollybush quarry, a source of valuable roadstone until fairly recently. Either path leads to the hamlet of Hollybush.

Unless it is a point of honour to scale every summit there is little to be gained from climbing Raggedstone Hill to the south of Hollybush; the recommended route is east along the A438 for 300yds (300m) and then into the lane on the right opposite the entrance to the quarry. Keep to the left when the path branches and follow a contour with the hill on the right. The way lies through woodland and emerges at the romantically named and picturesque hamlet of Whiteleaved Oak. Chase End Hill, the southernmost summit of the range, lies a short distance away. It is a fairly steep climb to an unfrequented spot, but worth it for the sense of achievement at the end of an exhilarating 10m (16km) walk.

A tour from the Malverns to Upton-on-Severn

Looking down from the hills at the open countryside stretching across the Severn it is difficult to believe that the area was once thick forest, part of the 7,000 acres (2,833 hectares) of woodland that surrounded the Malvern range. From the time of William the Conqueror onwards it was under direct royal jurisdiction with its own officers and laws. When the Earl of Gloucester married the daughter of Edward I, the forest was made over to him and became Malvern Chase. During the next 200 years large areas of the forest were cleared, parts were colonised, and by the time of Charles I a large number of people had claimed squatters' rights. In 1632 the position was regularised by royal decree; the king kept one third and the remainder was made available to the dwellers as 'commoners'.

There is little woodland left now but the area still has the unmistakable air of common land, with long straight roads linking the hills and the river. Something of the atmosphere of the Chase can be appreciated in the course of a drive from Great Malvern, across the hills and round the southern end to Upton-upon-Severn.

From the centre of Great Malvern take the A449 south through Malvern Wells. After passing through, watch out for a minor road descending steeply to the left and signposted Upton. Almost immediately after it you can turn into the drive of **St Wulfstan's Roman Catholic Church**, where Edward Elgar and his wife are buried in the churchyard. The A4104 now branches to the left, and a short distance along it is **Little Malvern Priory**, set back from the road on the right. It is a strange-looking building – the surviving tower and chancel of the former priory church. At the Dissolution the monastic buildings passed into private ownership (the adjacent Little Malvern Court incorporates some of them) but the usable parts of the church were made over to the parishioners. It has retained some of its medieval glass, the misericord stalls – unfortunately without most of their carving – and some tiles similar to those in Malvern Priory.

Return from here to the A449 which climbs up to Wynd's Point. From here the road descends into the Hereford-shire countryside, and there is a rather dull stretch before a left turn onto the A438 brings you to **Eastnor**. The main attraction here is the early nineteenth-century castle set beside a lake (open to the public), but the village itself is attractive with thatched cottages and a green. The church interior is very dark but notable for an ornate marble and gilt reredos and the alabaster memorial to the second Earl Somers.

After Eastnor the road crosses the hills again almost imperceptibly at Hollybush and emerges onto Malvern Chase. **Birts-morton Court** lies up a minor road on the left about 4m (6½km) later; it is semi-fortified with a moat and has many historical associations, including the fact that Cardinal Wolsey was family chaplain there as a young man. Much later William Huskisson, the early nineteenth-century politician, was born there. The Court is not open to the public but the exterior can be seen from the adjacent churchyard. There are some fine memorials in the church, among them a huge altar tomb lacking its effigy and an unusual wall monument to Admiral William Caldwell, showing his ship and an interesting collection of navigational instruments. The stained glass in the north chancel wall shows the murder of Thomas à Becket, to whom the church was dedicated before the Reformation.

After visiting Birtsmorton it is worth retracing the route for just a over a mile (1½km) and taking the B4208 north to Welland. The road crosses Castlemor-ton Common, a stretch of unenclosed country largely unaffected by modern development. Go straight through Welland and after a mile (1½km) turn right onto the minor road to **Hanley Swan**. The most interesting building here is not in the village itself but a mile to the north – the Roman Catholic church, which has a most sumptuous interior dating from 1846, the result of benefactions from the Hornyold family of nearby Blackmore Park.

Return to the crossroads at Hanley Swan, turn left onto the B4209 and right at the junction with the B4211. After half a mile (1km) the village of **Hanley Castle** lies just off the road to the right. It is rather genteel but undeniably attractive, with a tiny green and an intimate group of houses. There is not much sign of the castle now but parts of the medieval church survive, supplemented by a tower, chancel and north chapel built of brick in the seventeenth century. It contains some good monuments to the Lechmeres, the local family

associated with the village for centuries; most are in the chapel but there is one very distinguished memorial in the nave. The Victorian glass is unusually vivid, the reds and blues of the west window being almost flamboyant.

Outside, apart from the elaborately restored houses, is a picturesque pub called the Three Kings and, unexpectedly, a large secondary school. It was established by the Lechmeres as early as 1544, and as its varied buildings show it has been steadily enlarged since. Having served as a state grammar school for boys it has now become comprehensive and co-educational, a remarkable example of continuity and adaptation.

From here it is a short distance to Upton-upon-Severn, and the main car park is on the right as you enter the town.

Museum of Worcester Porcelain, Worcester

Places to Visit

IN AND AROUND WORCESTER

Visitor Centre

The Guildhall, High Street
☎ 01905 723471

The Cathedral

WR1 2LH
☎ 01905 28854
Architecture ranging from 11th to 16th centuries. Very fine crypt, tomb of King John, chantry of Prince Arthur (son of Henry VII).

City Museum and Art Gallery

Foregate Street WR1 1DT
☎ 01905 25371
Archaeology, natural history, geology, military collections, etc. Good permanent collection and touring exhibitions in Art Gallery.

The Commandery

In Sidbury WR1 2HU
☎ 01905 361821
Originally a 15th-century hospital with fine Great Hall. Houses museum of trades and industries and special display of Civil War items. Refreshments on canal bank.

Tudor House Heritage Centre

Friar Street WR1 2NA
☎ 01905 759344
Historic building of c.1550. Displays on Tudor life and Worcester's industrial and commercial heritage.

The Greyfriars (National Trust)

Friar Street WR1 2LZ
☎ 01905 23571
Timber-framed medieval merchant's house built in c.1480 with panelled rooms, antique textiles, rugs, carpets and furniture. Walled garden.

The Guildhall (Information Centre)

High Street
01905 723471
Elegant 18th-century civic building by local architect Thomas White. Celebrated facade, fine interior decoration, notable ballroom.

St Swithun's Church

The Shambles (adjacent to the Cross)
Built in 1736, one of the best examples in England of a Georgian city church. Interesting features include a pulpit with a carved pelican plucking its breast, a mayor's chair and a wrought iron civic sword rest. Currently redundant but visitors may obtain the key from the Tourist Information Centre in the Guildhall, High Street.

Royal Worcester Visitor Centre

Severn Street WR1 2NE
☎ 01905 21247
Site of famous pottery established in 1751. Centre is set among Victorian factory buildings. Guided tours, craftsmen at work, opportunity for plate painting. Royal Worcester bestware & seconds shops.

Places to Visit

Worcester Porcelain Museum

Severn Street WR1 2NE
☎ 01905 746000
Audio tour tells story of factory's history and workforce. Gallery displays illustrating vast range of designs.

Diglis Canal Basin

Riverside, reached by Severn Street. Junction of Worcester and Birmingham Canal with river Severn.

The Pump House Environment Centre

Gheluvelt Park, Barbourne
☎ 01905 730600
Former Victorian Waterworks building, converted into a community environment centre using a wide range of sustainable technologies. Focus on waste, water and energy conservation.

Worcestershire History Centre

Trinity Street
☎ 01905 765922
Facilities for family history research.

George Marshall Medical Museum

Charles Hastings Education Centre, Worcestershire Royal Hospital, Charles Hastings Way
☎ 01905 760738
Museum illustrating history of medicine, nursing and the associated health care professions, with particular reference to Worcester. 19th-century operating theatre and apothecary's shop.

Worcester Woods Country Park

Wildwood Drive WR5 2LG
☎ 01905 766493
110-acres (44.5 hectares) of ancient oak woodland and wildflower meadows. Circular walks, cafe, children's play area, picnic area.

Brockhampton Estate (National Trust)

Greenfields, Bringsty WR6 5TB
6m (10km) W of Worcester off A44
☎ 01885 488099
Medieval manor house on traditionally farmed estate. Over 5m (c.10km) of walks through park and woodland.

Spetchley Park Gardens

Spetchley WR5 1RS
3m (5km) from city centre on A422
☎ 01453 810303
House of the Berkeley family (not open to public). Magnificent gardens with rare trees and deer park. Plant sales.

The Elgar Birthplace Museum

Crown East Lane, Lower Broadheath WR2 6RH
☎ 01905 333224
Cottage in which Elgar was born in 1857. Collection of scores, photographs, letters, personal mementoes, etc.

Worcester Three Choirs Festival

☎ 01905 616200
info.worcester@3choirs.org

IN AND AROUND MALVERN

Visitor Information

21 Church Street
☎ 01684 892289

The Priory

Norman origin but mainly the result of 15th-century rebuilding. Splendid interior, with 15th-century glass, misericords and outstanding collection of medieval tiles.

Malvern Museum

Priory Gatehouse WR14 3ES
☎ 01684 567811
Mainly local history, including the water cure, Elgar and Morgan cars.

Malvern Theatres

Grange Road
☎ 01684 892277
Leading regional theatre and entertainments venue.

Malvern Showground

Malvern WR13 6NW
☎ 01684 584900

St Ann's Well

Signposted from Malvern Centre. Traditional source of Malvern water; interesting 19th-century building. cafe.

Worcestershire Beacon

Highest point of Malvern Hills with superb views. Accessible from many points, including St Ann's Well.

Herefordshire Beacon

Spectacular Iron Age fort, accessible from car park at Wynds Point near Little Malvern.

Little Malvern Priory

On A4104, 4m (6½km) S of Great Malvern
☎ 01684 892988
Interesting priory church, adjacent to **Little Malvern Court**, which has a Prior's Hall of c.1480, displays of vestments, paintings and 10-acres (4hectare) of gardens.

St Wulfstan's Roman Catholic Church

On A449 S of Malvern Wells
Grave of Sir Edward Elgar and his wife in churchyard.

Newland Church and Almshouses

On A449, 3m (5km) N of Great Malvern
Interesting group of 19th-century almshouses with church of same period in French style.

Eastnor Castle

HR8 1RL On A438, 2m (3km) E of Ledbury
☎ 01531 633160
Castle built in 1814. Pictures, furniture, armour, tapestries, etc. Fine grounds with large lake. Children's attractions.

4. Upton-upon-Severn to Gloucester and the Severn Vale

For many visitors, **Upton-upon-Severn** will prove to be the most attractive of the Severnside towns. It has much in common with Bewdley both in geography and history; its period of greatest prosperity was in the eighteenth century when it rivalled Bewdley and Worcester as a river port, but unlike them it had little to fall back on when the river trade died. Consequently it became a modest country town and has retained much of its village atmosphere.

Upton-on-Severn to Gloucester

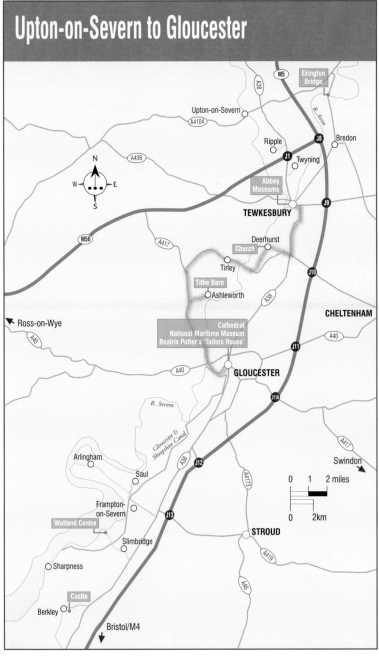

A walk around Upton-upon-Severn

Walk from the car park to the bridge. The present haunched cantilever bridge was built in 1940, although one of its predecessors played an important part in the Civil War during the preliminaries to the Battle of Worcester. The bridge was the only one between Worcester and Tewkesbury, and had been breached in order to deny it to the Parliamentary army, but someone had been careless enough to leave a plank lying across and the entire force of Ironsides was able to get over. The present bridge provides a good view of a miniature waterfront, where a walk around the town can begin.

At one time Upton was noted for its innumerable inns, and you pass two of them, the Plough and the King's Arms, before reaching a group of eighteenth-century warehouses that have been modernised but left with sufficient character to preserve the wharf atmosphere. There are always plenty of boats tied up along here, one of the permanent fixtures being a big river barge. By continuing along the riverside it is possible to see some of the interesting houses further downstream. The **Malt House** is probably the best – a very impressive Georgian mansion with beautifully detailed windows – but there is fine brickwork and unusual embellishment in an earlier building called the King's Stable just beyond. Severn House and Old Walls, both of the eighteenth century, complete the row.

Return towards the town but this time go along **Dunn's Lane**, which passes behind the warehouses. At its start is Waterside House, another fine Georgian structure, but the main attraction of Dunn's Lane is the group of cottages behind the Swan Inn. They are rather genteel now, and it is difficult to imagine this as a dirty and noisy alley as it was in the late eighteenth century, or in the 1830s when it was the centre of an outbreak of cholera.

Dunn's Lane leads into the **High Street**, with the timber-framed Anchor Inn on the corner; the large gable over the adjacent shop gives its date as 1601. The inn is the first in a line of harmonious old buildings on the left-hand side of the High Street, including the elegant White Lion Hotel and the Talbot Head Hotel with its very distinctive windows. High Street extends into Old Street, though if you have time it is rewarding to turn left into Court Street and look at Court Row.

Old Street is narrow and its attractions are less obvious, but there is much to enjoy in the details of these unpretentious buildings that provide such a rich variety of facades. They are mainly Georgian and Victorian, though No. 51 is an interesting timber-framed house of the seventeenth century, and tucked away behind wrought-iron gates just before it is a handsome Baptist chapel of 1734. At the end of Old Street the town suddenly comes to an end and the view is dominated by the lofty spire of the 'new' parish church, built in 1879 to replace the smaller one by the bridge. Unfortunately its Bath stone has obstinately refused to weather attractively, while the interior is solid and even sumptuous without having any features that could be called distinguished.

Return down Old Street and turn left at the crossroads into **New Street**.

There are some rather over-prettified shops with the date 1668 on the left, but once again the attraction lies in the variegated range of frontages on both sides. At the bottom on the left is a plaque recording the fact that the 'ducking pond' for scolds was situated nearby.

As you return to the High Street and walk towards the river the most prominent feature ahead is Upton's famous landmark, the **Bell Tower**. In appearance it is a conventional church tower with an incongruous cupola on the top (hence its local name – the Pepper Pot), and the odd combination is explained by the fact that in 1754 a new nave and chancel were added to the fourteenth-century tower and the cupola was designed as a finishing touch to the church's new classical appearance. After the construction of the new and larger church the old one became redundant and the nave and chancel were removed in the 1930s. The Tower now houses some informative displays of local history and geography.

The churchyard has been left as an open space with the old market cross looking down on the High Street at one end. There is a particularly interesting row of houses on the opposite side of Church Street, notably the well-restored Cromwell Cottages, late sixteenth-century and close-studded. Finally, on returning to the car park, note the attractive row of eighteenth-century cottages in the road leading to the bridge.

There are two easy riverside walks from Upton. The first follows the start of the town walk along the quay, but the lane by the river soon becomes a footpath that runs for two miles along the bank before turning to join a track at Buryend Farm for the return to town. The second begins on the other side of the bridge and follows the river for two miles northward, passing Severn End, the home of the Lechmere family, on the opposite bank.

On to Tewkesbury

The route now is into Gloucestershire by way of the A38, reached at a junction to the east of Upton. There is not much to stop for during the six-mile (10km) run to **Tewkesbury**, which arrives suddenly since there are no suburbs in this direction. Once across the Avon bridge you are in the middle of the town. The main car park is most easily reached by driving the length of the main street, turning left at the junction with the A438 and then watching for a sign a few hundred yards along on the left.

This is where the Avon joins the Severn, and medieval Tewkesbury was consequently a place of some importance. It had strong royal connections during its early history and was the scene of a major battle in 1471 during the Wars of the Roses. Economically it prospered on the wool trade and the busy commerce of the rivers. The confluence of the rivers led to Tewkesbury suffering some of the worst effects of the flooding which occurred across Gloucestershire, and affected much of the area covered in this book, in the summer of 2007. Nowadays the most obvious sign of the town's historic status is the Abbey, which still dominates the western end of the town and is the natural starting point for a walk.

Tewkesbury Abbey

Above: 'Out of the Hat', Heritage and visitor centre, Church Street, Tewkesbury and (below) Lilleys Alley

A walk around Tewkesbury

Its sheer size and grandeur make it difficult to think of **Tewkesbury Abbey** in other than cathedral terms, although it is technically a parish church, purchased by the Corporation from Henry VIII at the Dissolution. Built by Robert Fitzhamon in the very early twelfth century with imported Caen stone, it has undergone several restorations since, but nothing has detracted from the basic simplicity of the cruciform exterior, graced with one of England's finest Norman towers.

Simplicity and strength are also the first impressions on entering the nave. The arcades are supported on huge round pillars and the vaulting above is functional rather than delicate. Since there is no intervening screen the contrast between the grey nave and the bright colour and light tracery of the choir roof is very striking. Almost all the interior embellishment has been concentrated at the east end, where there is a wealth of historical interest. Instead of the usual principal window, the east wall contains an arc of seven windows with magnificent fourteenth-century glass paid for by the widow of Hugh le Despenser. The Despensers and their complicated network of relatives had close associations with the Abbey, and they are commemorated by a famous group of chantries in the choir. Most date from the same period – the turn of the fourteenth century – and are encrusted with unbelievably elaborate filigree ornament.

At the back of the high altar a series of small chapels are ranged against the east wall, and among the interesting memorials is one grisly example portraying the partly decomposed body of an abbot. Here too is a sixteenth-century 'Armada chest', designed to receive contributions towards the upkeep of the navy and fitted with an intricate lock that covers most of the lid. The older of the two organs dates from 1610. It was originally made for Magdalen College, Oxford, and was later presented to Oliver Cromwell, giving rise to a story that Milton played it at Hampton Court.

Now walk down Mill Street, directly opposite the abbey gates. There are two notable buildings at the bottom by the river. The nineteenth-century **mill** (now a restaurant) formed part of the setting of Mrs Craik's once-famous *John Halifax, Gentleman*, a novel with many other local associations. Close by is the attractive rough-hewn **granary**, originally part of the Abbey buildings and now restored. Back at the top of Mill Street, the **Bell Hotel** of about 1696 accommodated Mrs Craik while she was writing her novel, but rather more pleasing to the eye jaded by so much timber-framing is the simple and elegant former **National School** of 1813 that stands nearby.

The centre of Tewkesbury is Y-shaped, which makes a circular tour difficult, but most of the interesting buildings lie in Church Street and High Street which run parallel to the old course of the Avon. Running behind the frontages are a number of alleyways that once teemed with squalid life but now provide quiet oases away from the traffic. One of these is almost immediately on the left as you set off down Church Street. **Old Baptist Chapel**

Court once contained a number of tiny medieval cottages, and in the 1620s three of them were combined into one of the earliest of England's Nonconformist chapels, now restored to its original form.

A unique survival on the other side of Church Street is the range of tiny fifteenth-century shops known as **Abbey Cottages**. They were basically primitive houses, transformed each day into shops by letting down the window shutters to form counters, and one of them has been left as a reconstruction. A Georgian house sits strangely in the middle of the row, but it is remarkable that so many of the cottages survived. At the far end of them the **John Moore Museum** has been established to commemorate the well-known local novelist, author of the *Brensham Trilogy*.

Interesting buildings come thick and fast as you walk towards the Cross. Most of them are timber-framed and of a kind that reflect urban prosperity rather than simple living. Craik House, the Old Hat Shop, Cross House, Warwick House and the Berkeley Arms all stand within a short distance of each other, while Lilley's Alley and Ancill's Court reveal the rewards of exploring behind the main street. All this antiquity throws the Georgian facade of the **Royal Hop Pole Hotel** into greater prominence; apart from being extremely handsome (and older than it looks) it was the hotel chosen by Dickens for Mr Pickwick to lodge at.

At the Cross the forks of the Y branch off, with Church Street continuing to the left and becoming High Street. It is impossible to detail all the attractions along here. The guidebooks point with pride to obvious showpieces like the superb seven-bay **Swan Hotel**, the precariously-jettied **'House of the Nodding Gables'**, the **Old Fleece**, the **Ancient Grudge** restaurant and the **Tudor House Hotel**. They are certainly fine, but they distract attention from more modest buildings of great individuality.

The discerning visitor will want to look out for the late eighteenth-century **Town Hall**, which is surprisingly small, built of sandstone, decorated with pilasters and topped off with a cupola. Next door is a spectacular piece of fakery that has genuine claims to distinction, while on the other side of the road Auriol House (1606) has a tall, slender frontage with a two-storey bow window. A hundred yards (100m) further up is a most impressive Georgian mansion with a central entrance arch and Venetian windows above it on two floors.

At the far end of the High Street a left turn called Quay Street provides a vista of big riverside buildings. On the right is the only uncompromisingly modern building in the town centre – the **Roses Theatre**, which achieved a sad niche in show-business history as the place where comedian Eric Morecambe suffered a fatal collapse after a performance in May 1984. The **Black Bear Inn**, reputedly the oldest pub in Gloucestershire, marks the end of the street, and by turning left here you reach **King John's Bridge**, first constructed in 1197 and much altered since.

Return now to the High Street, walk up Sun Street past the theatre and turn right into Oldbury Road, where you pass **Holy Trinity Church**. This is another building not mentioned in the guidebooks, but its rather ordinary brick facade conceals a most elegant early nineteenth-century church, characteristically spacious and uncluttered. It is the only Anglican church apart from the Abbey, and in its heyday it was obviously the place of worship preferred by the humbler section of the population; to accommodate them it was necessary to have two tiers of galleries. Follow Oldbury Road to its end and you emerge into Tewkesbury's third main thoroughfare, **Barton Street**.

The architecture here is on a smaller scale and more humdrum in character; mainly Georgian and Victorian but none the worse for that. A notable pair of half-timbered houses have been converted to form a **museum and information centre**. Further back towards the Cross on the left is a former Baptist church that looks as if it might once have been a small coaching inn. It faces a line of small shops with faded but interesting early Victorian frontages. The tour is completed by walking back along Church Street to the Abbey.

On to Gloucester (with diversions)

Leave Tewkesbury on the A38 and after three miles (5km) turn right onto the B4213. After another half-mile (1km) a minor road branches off right to **Deerhurst**. The village itself is not especially remarkable but it was of some importance in Saxon times; King Edmund and King Canute met here in 1016 to sign a treaty redrawing the boundary between Saxons and Danes. The reason for its pre-eminence was its

priory, probably founded in the seventh century and destined to become the leading religious foundation of the kingdom of Hwicce. Its influence declined with the foundation of abbeys at Tewkesbury and Gloucester, and at the Dissolution it was sold to the Throckmorton family. The **priory church**, however, was converted for parish use, and thus it can claim to be among the very oldest churches in Britain (some say the oldest).

Saxon herringbone masonry is visible on the outside and the interior shows evidence of several stages of building around the ancient nave that is the original core. But there are other interesting features apart from its architectural development. The richly carved Saxon font is the finest to be seen in this part of England. The memorial brass to Sir John Cassy and his wife (c.1400) is one of only two in the country to show a pet dog with a name – Tirri. Eight pews have also survived from the fifteenth century, but perhaps the most striking evidence of continuity of worship here is the arrangement of pews around the altar for the celebration of Holy Communion in the puritan style.

Visible from the church gate and reached along a short lane is **Odda's Chapel**. It was discovered in 1885 within the framework of the house to which it is still attached, and a memorial stone dates it precisely at 1056. Barn-like in form, it consists of a surprisingly lofty nave and a small chancel in rough stone. Earl Odda was a friend of Edward the Confessor, and the Chapel was erected in memory of his brother.

The minor road out of Deerhurst to the south rejoins the B4213 near the

Gloucester farmers' market

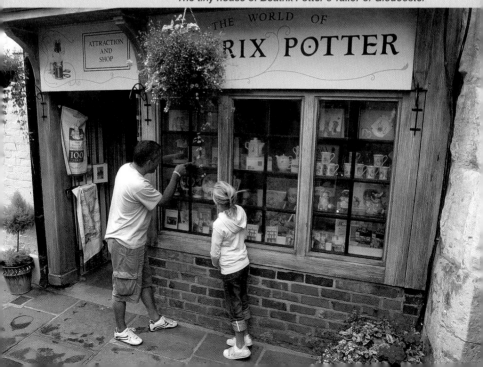

The tiny house of Beatrix Potter's Tailor of Gloucester

point where it crosses the Severn over the lonely Haw Bridge. The countryside here is dotted with wooded hills and threaded with intricate, narrow lanes linking small hamlets, and to avoid getting lost it is best to follow the road to its junction with the B4211 and on to the A417. A mile or so (2km) later you reach Hartpury where a left turn leads to **Ashleworth**.

This appears to be a conventional village, but if you turn down past the village green you arrive at the ancient riverside settlement. Very little remains of the once-important quay (flood banks have displaced it) and the ferry no longer runs. The former waterside inn now appears to be a private house. But three interesting buildings have survived close to the river. The tithe barn of about 1500 is like a smaller version of the better-known barns at Bredon and Littleton, although it has no upper storey; it has been discreetly restored by the National Trust and retains its original appearance. Set back behind it is Ashleworth Court, a former monastic building of the fifteenth century and still distinctly ecclesiastical in character, with a big entrance arch and a variety of window shapes. The adjacent church has some herringbone masonry and a magnificent old entrance door, but its outstanding feature (apart from what appears to be the worst stained glass in Gloucestershire) is the rood screen in the south aisle, complete with loft floor and steps for access built into the wall. At the west end of the aisle is a huge royal coat of arms of the Tudor period.

As you approach the city centre from this direction you will see direction signs to the St Oswald's park and ride point, and you may consider this option preferable to negotiating the city's streets.

Gloucester

Gloucester has three distinct personalities. It is a cathedral city, a modern commercial centre and a port. Like Worcester, it has suffered from major development which has largely destroyed its medieval character, but it is rather more fortunate in what has been left. The grid of its pre-Norman street plan still exists, and the Cross is still the junction of streets named Northgate, Eastgate, Southgate and Westgate.

In fact Northgate Street and Southgate Street probably follow the line of a Roman road. A legionary fortress, established here soon after the main Roman invasion, was developed into an elaborate civilian settlement and received official town status as Colonia Nervia Glevensis at the end of the first century. The title 'Colonia' indicates a place of considerable importance and there is reason to believe that it was one of the most impressive of the Roman communities, although growth was evidently stunted by the development of nearby Cirencester.

At the beginning of the tenth century, Queen Aethelflaed of Mercia encouraged the foundation of a new settlement within the Roman defences. In the next 200 years it became a centre of royal power and a meeting place for the king and his council; the Domesday Book was finally planned here in 1085. Four years later work began on a new church for the monastery, the fourth to be built at Gloucester and the basis of the present cathedral. Although the Abbey church acquired cathedral status in 1540, Gloucester's prosperity was largely the result of industrial development in the late eighteenth century, helped later by the creation of an extensive complex of inland docks that made possible a thriving timber and corn trade.

A walk around Gloucester

The tour of the town centre which follows starts at the west end of Westgate Street, at its junction with The Quay, but since it is a circular walk it can be started at any point on the route. (The Docks are not included in this walk, but a suggested tour is described later)

As you walk up Westgate Street the first building of note is the distinguished timber-framed house on the right. This is **Bishop Hooper's Lodging**, the house where a Protestant Bishop of Gloucester reputedly spent his last night before being burnt at the stake in 1555. It is a well-restored example of a sixteenth-century group of town houses, now used to accommodate a folk museum. Opposite is **St Nicholas's Church** with its unusual truncated spire ,and next to it the elaborate Georgian facade of a house that in fact dates from the sixteenth century.

Take the first turning on the left after the church. It is a lane leading to **St Mary's Square**, a modern but attractive development incorporating a large Victorian monument to Bishop Hooper and the church of St Mary de Lode (the church is normally kept locked).What catches the eye here is the ancient **St Mary's Gateway** leading into the cathedral precincts. It is an elaborate thirteenth-century structure with stone vaulting, and picturesque houses flank it on each side. You pass under it to enter **College Green**, which is worth a tour to study the varied architecture ranging from the sixteenth to the eighteenth centuries. By walking round the west end of the cathedral to Miller's Green it is possible to see the **Parliament Room**, a fifteenth-century hall grafted on to an earlier stone building. It was originally a monastic house and received its name after a meeting of Parliament there in 1378.

The cathedral itself was begun in 1089 and its nave still retains the enormous strength of the Norman period. The apparent contrast between the plain round pillars and the decorated arches is explained by the fact that new arcading was constructed in the thirteenth century.As usual some of the most interesting monuments are to be found here.A splendid coloured memorial of the early seventeenth century to Thomas Machen and his wife shows seven sons and six daughters mourning them, the younger ones squeezed in rather perfunctorily.There is a stone to Edward Jenner, the pioneer of vaccination, and nearby Sir Onesiphorus Paul is commemorated by a monument that describes his impressive record as a prison reformer. However, the most striking memorial is probably that to Sarah Morley, who died after giving birth to a child during a voyage from India in 1784. The crisp carving by Flaxman shows angels lifting her from the sea with her child in her arms.

After the sobriety of the nave a blaze of colour greets you as you move into the south transept. The tiny chapel of St John the Baptist has been brilliantly restored with medieval tiles on the floor, painted emblems on the woodwork and a reredos encrusted with bright colour and gilding. There is further wall painting and another fine reredos in the nearby St Andrew's Chapel, and art of another kind in the painted table tomb of Alderman Blackleech and his wife. This transept is also of great architectural significance in that it was one of the earliest attempts (possibly the first) at what has come to be known as the Perpendicular style.

In the choir, a series of slender columns supporting intricate tracery contrast strongly with the nave and raise the roof 20 feet (6m) higher. At the west-end the organ pipes are finely displayed above the screen, decorated with seventeenth-century painting, while the east end is dominated by the largest stained-glass window in England. This is an astounding creation, 78ft (24m) high and 38ft (11½m) wide, dating from 1349 and designed as a triptych with its sides turning in. Its main theme is the Coronation of the Blessed Virgin Mary, and beneath the main group of figures are depicted various kings, saints and martyrs, while lower panels show the shields of many of the knights who fought in the Hundred Years War. Not even the tall and exuberant reredos can detract from the impact of the window. The isolated tomb before the high altar is that of Robert, eldest son of William the Conqueror, whose wooden effigy leaves him in an excruciating cross-legged position. Back in the south ambulatory is a remarkable example of fifteenth-century joinery – a vast semicircular cope chest.

The size of the east window is even more vividly appreciated as you pass directly beneath it to the entrance of the Lady Chapel. This is built on a large scale, but extensive Victorian restoration has not left much of outstanding interest, apart from the east window where the jumbled glass dates from the fifteenth century. Beneath it the plain reredos is decorated with modern relief panels. There are two or three striking memorials, the most grandiose being to John Powell, a judge who died in 1713.

The main feature of the north ambulatory is the tomb of Edward II, whose body was brought here following his murder at Berkeley Castle. The beautifully carved effigy is contained within an intricate stone canopy. Close by, in a wall case, a simple stone cross is an unpretentious reminder of an almost forgotten episode in the Korean War, when a battalion of the Gloucestershire Regiment made a heroic stand at the Imjin river against impossible odds. The cross was carved by their commander, Col JP Came VC, during his period of captivity after the action.

From the north transept, containing another remarkable aldermanic memorial of 1615, it is possible to walk into the cloisters, well worth visiting for their elegant fan vaulting, the earliest surviving example of the style. The Chapter House stands on the east side, but perhaps more notable is a rare example in the north cloister of a monks' lavatorium.

Gloucester Cathedral and (below) the cloisters

After visiting the cathedral, the way back to Westgate Street is down College Street, immediately opposite the main door. On leaving the precincts you see the remains of the ancient principal entrance, **King Edward's Gate**. At the end of College Street, note the imposing piece of mock-Tudor on the corner before turning left. Do not miss the next alleyway, because halfway along it is the curious little house (open to the public) chosen by Beatrix Potter as the home of one of her best-known characters, the Tailor of Gloucester.

Just before reaching the Cross, Gloucester's commercial hub, turn left into **St John's Lane**. The church at the top has a typically eighteenth-century appearance and an interior of appropriate elegance, although the tower and spire are fourteenth-century. The lane runs into Northgate Street, and away from the Cross, in Hare Lane, Sainsbury's remarkable mural and the medieval buildings on each side of the shop should not be missed. There are two good pubs along here too – the immense **Tabard** in lordly mock-Tudor and the smaller **Imperial**, with an outstanding Victorian facade full of ornate patterns and bright green tiling. The Imperial may be preferred to the much-praised **New Inn**, which is on the left as you walk towards the Cross. It is a fifteenth-century pub with a false front and a picturesque creeper-clad courtyard, but the profusion of signs and olde-worlde decorations give it a rather artificial appearance. At the Cross, turn left along Eastgate Street to see the splendid Victorian **Guildhall** (now an arts venue) in a restrained Italian style, carefully matched by the two adjacent

bank buildings. Unless you want to visit the two large shopping malls on each side of Eastgate Street you should turn back to the Cross.

Amid all the nondescript modern development at the Cross, the tower of **St Michael's Church** is retained on one corner. By passing beneath it and turning left into Southgate Street you reach one of the quaint attractions of Gloucester, the **clockmaker's shop** with a colourful line of carved figures over the window. They represent John Bull, Father Time, an Irishman, a Scotsman and a Welshwoman, and they each strike a bell as the clock chimes. The fine Jacobean house almost next door was the town residence of the Berkeley family.

A handsome range of buildings further down Southgate Street on the right includes the house where **Robert Raikes**, philanthropist and pioneer of Sunday schools, lived from 1768 to 1801. Its timbering blends harmoniously with the adjacent County Hotel. Redundancy has hit most of the city's old parish churches, but a glorious exception stands almost opposite, and it is worth reserving a generous amount of time to look round **St Mary de Crypt**.

It is an example of the Perpendicular style widely adopted after its introduction in the cathedral, although it has been much restored and altered both in the nineteenth century and in recent years. It stands in an attractive setting with big chestnut trees and is a welcome refuge from the traffic. The high arcades and tower arches give an unexpectedly spacious atmosphere to the nave, and the long chancel is equally impressive. The clerestory here was a sixteenth-century addition and the Victorians added the screen, the east window (a copy of medieval glass) and the mosaic reredos, but it all fits harmoniously together. The outstanding feature is the painting on the north wall of the chancel, uncovered in 1842 and showing the Adoration of the Magi as seen by an anonymous sixteenth-century artist. Following skilful restoration enough remains to show that it was a rich and accomplished piece of work that must have cost a considerable sum, but there is no hint of the benefactor who paid for it.

The flanking chapels have some interesting monuments and there are good brasses in the north transept and aisle. The staircase in this aisle leads to the upper floor of the old schoolroom next door that was built in 1539 and now serves as the church hall. Another famous figure associated with St Mary's was George Whitefield, the inspirational eighteenth-century preacher and colleague of John Wesley, and one of the most attractive things at the church is the tiny, tulip-shaped font at which he was baptised. He delivered his first sermons here and the pulpit that he used has been restored.

The path behind the church leads to **Greyfriars**, a thirteenth-century foundation with a church of which the nave and north aisle survive, incongruously surrounded by uninspired modern building. The path emerges into Brunswick Road close to the **City Museum and Art Gallery**. Towards the bottom of Brunswick Road there is a right turn into Parliament Street, where the mixture of modest cottages of great charm stand on the fringe of the dock area and have a waterfront atmosphere about them.

When you reach Southgate Street again, cross into Commercial Road, where there is a good view of one of the dock basins. The classical building on the left here is the former **Custom House** (now a military museum) and immediately opposite is Ladybellgate Street, which looks unpromising until you reach **Blackfriars** (Sunday opening). It is claimed to be the best-preserved Dominican friary in Britain and was founded at about the same time as the rival Greyfriars. Surrounding buildings make it difficult to appreciate the layout but the significant remains are the church and the cloisters. At the top of Ladybellgate Street the house of the same name presents a most imposing front, but its old grandeur has now been neutralised by office blocks on a much more brutal scale. Built in 1705, it was later the home of the Raikes family. Its fine interior has been restored in exceptional fashion by the Civic Trust. Two other superb eighteenth-century houses, **Bearland House** and **Bearland Lodge**, can be seen by turning left into Longsmith Street.

Berkeley Street leads back from here towards the cathedral, a good example of what can be done to blend old and new architecture. It is an attractive little pedestrian precinct with the seventeenth-century Fountain Inn towards the top. At Westgate Street turn left. Almost immediately you pass the **Shire Hall**, much altered since its construction in the early nineteenth century but still retaining Robert Smirke's big columned portico.

From here it is a short distance back to your starting point in Westgate Street. The tour will have revealed the extent to which Gloucester has suffered from recent development; as at Worcester there are a good many old buildings remaining, but they have lost their characteristic surroundings and tend to be isolated among modern structures on a totally different scale.

Luckily the same cannot be said about the docks, which remain a priceless asset with unique potential for an inland town, now being realised.

Gloucester Docks

Elizabeth I officially authorised the port in 1580, but there is evidence that the Romans had a quay here, and there was a good deal of water traffic in the middle ages on a channel (now vanished) that lay to the east of the present course of the river. The port was too close to the rapidly developing Bristol to be really prosperous, and the extensive complex owes its existence to the **Gloucester and Sharpness Canal**. This major waterway, designed to obviate the navigational difficulties of the river, was started in 1793, but a series of financial problems and changes of plan delayed its completion until 1827.

The resulting ease of access for large ships enabled Gloucester to become a major distribution point for Irish wheat and Baltic timber. The original docks were expanded in 1849 and 1892, while the construction of deep-water docks at Sharpness led to an increase in barge traffic. In recent years, however, Avonmouth has monopolised the new container traffic and little commercial activity goes on now at Gloucester, but adaptation for leisure and cultural purposes has ensured the survival of much of the fine architectural legacy of the complex.

National Waterways Museum

The **Docks** area is best viewed as a series of vistas from the perimeter roads, and a convenient place to start is the old Custom House in Commercial Road. It stands close to the original main entrance to the docks, and despite its 1840 date it has all the elegance of the eighteenth century. The big flour mills close to it date from 1850. Near the junction of Commercial Road and Southgate Street is a vantage point with a commanding view of the Victoria Dock of 1849. The three main warehouses that line it are appropriately called the Victoria, the Britannia and the Albert and they were all built for the wheat trade, although this dock was also used for loading salt from Droitwich, one of the few products exported from Gloucester by sea.

Now walk down the lower end of Southgate Street and turn in at the next dock entrance past the classical weigh bridge office to appreciate the impressive solidity and pleasing proportions of the warehouses and marvel at the variety of craft in the basin. Here too is the little **Mariners' Chapel** of 1849.

Continue down Southgate Street and take the next turning on the right (Llanthony Road), which brings you to the lifting bridge at the point where the canal enters the docks. From here you have the most striking view of all, along the length of the main basin with the earliest of the warehouses at the top end. It dates from 1826, and those ranged down the right-hand side were added in the 1840s. In the other direction the canal (the widest in Britain when it was opened) stretches away past Baker's Quay and the Pillar Warehouse.

A carpark enables you to explore more on foot. Look out for the Na-tional Maritime Museum near to the Mariners' Chapel. It fills one of the warehouses and is well worth a visit, being fascinating for children and adults alike.

Continue along Llanthony Road (the pleasant grounds of Llanthony Priory are on your left) and turn right into Severn Road, where the river appears on the left, looking oddly irrelevant. This is not the most pleasant road in Gloucester but it provides further views across the main basin and leads to a big warehouse which has been converted into an **Antiques Centre**; immediately after it, cross the narrow bridge over the channel giving access to the Severn from the docks. The right turn here leads back to Commercial Road and the starting point of the walk.

The Severn Vale

Much of Gloucestershire is taken up by the Cotswolds, to the east of the Severn, and the Forest of Dean, to the west. Lying between them is the narrow strip of low-lying riverside land called **Severn Vale**, which, despite receiving less notice in the tourist literature, is a most rewarding area to visit.

For centuries the Vale has been prosperous agricultural country, largely undisturbed except for the cutting of the Gloucester and Sharpness Canal and, more recently, the building of various industrial installations on the shore of the estuary itself. 'Shore' is a more appropriate word than 'bank' here, because after Gloucester the Severn begins to widen impressively, its narrow navigational channel threading vast areas of sandbank and mudflat.

The atmosphere can be sampled by leaving Gloucester on the A38 and turning right onto the B4071 about six miles (10km) after leaving the city to reach **Frampton-on-Severn**. Strung out on each side of one of the biggest village greens in Britain, it is generally acknowledged as the Vale's most attractive village. Frampton Court, built in the 1730s, dominates the eastern side of the green. The home of the Clifford family, it offers superior bed-and-breakfast, and its gardens can be visited by appointment – well worth the effort, because the extensive grounds include a canal, an astonishing 'Gothick' orangery and a seventeenth-century dovecote. Facing the Court is Frampton Manor, a fine timber-framed house, and a long row of variegated houses, some extremely picturesque, but others nondescript enough to save the village from undue prettiness. A walk to the extreme end of the long lane is justified, not only to admire the assorted building styles but to visit the church, which has a rare example of a lead font.

Continuing along the B4071 you enter the 'Arlingham Peninsula', around which the Severn makes its last spectacular meander. Many of the cottages here are built in the distinctive pinkish-grey local brick, seen to advantage at **Saul** where there is a concentration of former boatmen's houses. The long-disused **Stroudwater Canal** joined the Severn at **Framilode**, just to the north of Saul; it was built to connect with the Thames and Severn Canal and was the final link in a waterway that connected England's two biggest rivers. It is still possible to trace its course in broken stretches beside the River Frome, which also joins the Severn at Framilode.

These little river and canal communities must have been rough places at one time, and their churches were built late. Those at Fretherne and Framilode date from the middle of the nineteenth century and are not of great interest, although the position of Framilode church, alone and right on the edge of the mudflats, is romantic. **Arlingham church**, however, should not be

The Severn Bore

The Severn Bore is a tidal wave caused by the fact that the River Severn experiences an almost uniquely high tide. The difference between the lowest and highest tidal levels on any day can be as much as 50 feet (15m), so it is not surprising that the exceptionally high incoming tides that occur several times a year produce spectacular results when the tidal inrush meets the water coming downstream. A wave that can reach 6 or 7feet (2m) in height is forced upstream. The Bore cannot be precisely forecast, but if you happen to be in the area when it occurs you will learn about it from local publicity. A popular viewing point is the bridge at **Over**, on the northern outskirts of Gloucester, and a good alternative is **Minsterworth**, an isolated village off the A48, 6 miles (10km) west of Gloucester. It has a riverside pub, which can be a great comfort when estimated timings for the Bore prove less than accurate.

missed; it has medieval glass, eighteenth-century chandeliers and some notable monuments.

Those who enjoy solitary walking will note that there are paths beginning and ending at Saul that make possible a ramble round the shore of the peninsula, with a distant prospect of the Forest of Dean on the other side of the river. Another lonely walk begins at Splatt Bridge near Frampton church and can be continued south to the **Wildfowl and Wetlands Centre** at **Slimbridge**. It is a rather longer journey for motorists, who need to return to the A38 and drive 3 miles (5km) to the Slimbridge turn. The Centre, founded by Sir Peter Scott as the Wildfowl Trust, is home to the world's largest collection of ducks, geese and swans, including rare and endangered species.

Return to the A38, and after six miles (10km) turn off for **Berkeley**, where the **castle** is the Vale's other celebrated attraction. The town has never developed into the thriving place it might have been if the builders of the canal to Gloucester had carried out their original intention of linking it with the Severn here. As it is, Berkeley has remained a large village with an enhanced status derived from the castle. There is some pleasant Georgian architecture and the fine Berkeley Arms Hotel, while the **parish church** is worth visiting for the tombs in the Berkeley Chapel, and the hut nearby in which **Edward Jenner** conducted his first experiments in smallpox vaccination. A small Jenner museum has been established in Church Lane, in the cottage he gave to his first 'guinea pig'.

The Berkeleys have been referred to several times already in connection with Worcester and Gloucester. The family is one of the few that can trace its line reliably back to the Norman Conquest and possibly even further, and it has been in continuous occupation of the castle here since the time of Henry II. Since that time, the castle has undergone many alterations and extensions, and it is now a complex range of buildings. The Norman keep still stands, but is rather outclassed by the fourteenth-century additions, in particular the chapel and magnificent Great Hall. It was at this time that Edward II was murdered in grisly fashion here, and his dungeon can be visited today. There is a great deal to see here, and plenty of time should be reserved for your visit.

Wildfowl & Wetlands Centre, Slimbridge

Places to Visit

IN AND AROUND UPTON-ON-SEVERN

Tourist Information Centre
4 High Street
☎ 01684 594200

Tiltridge Vineyard
Upper Hook Road, Upton
☎ 01684 592906
Award-winning white wine producers.
Tasting and shop.

Croome Park (National Trust)
6 miles (10km) NE of Upton off A38
at Severn Stoke
01905 371006
The first complete landscape project
by Capability Brown.

IN AND AROUND TEWKESBURY

Tewkesbury Town Museum
64 Barton Street
☎ 01684 292277
Local life and history including Battle
of Tewkesbury.

The John Moore Countryside Museum
41 Church Street
☎ 01684 292277
Commemorates novelist who set
his stories in the Tewkesbury area.
Natural history, domestic bygones,
farming, wildlife sculptures.

The Abbey
One of Britain's finest Norman
towers. Splendid interior containing
fourteenth-century glass, notable
chantry tombs, 17th-century organ

Old Baptist Chapel
Off Church Street
Restored chapel that was originally
a 15th-century house. First used by
Baptists in 1623.

Deerhurst Church
2 miles (3km) S of Tewkesbury off
A38
Thought to be the oldest church
in England to which a date can be
assigned. Interesting progression
of architecture from Saxon times
onwards. Unusual arrangement of
pews around altar.

Odda's Chapel
Near Deerhurst Church
Saxon chapel of 1056, discovered
within farmhouse.

IN AND AROUND GLOUCESTER

Visitor Information
Southgate Street
☎ 01452 396572

Gloucester Cathedral
Norman nave with massive columns
and the world-famous early fan-
vaulting. Glazed cloisters, with
monks' lavatorium. Largest stained-
glass window in England.

Places to Visit

Gloucester Guildhall

23 Eastgate Street GL1 1NS
☎ 01452 503050
Arts and entertainment venue. Art gallery, cinema, theatre. Cafe bar.

Llanthony Secunda Priory

Off Llanthony Road
☎ 01452 396620
Attractive park and ruins of Llanthony Secunda Priory. Formerly a community of Augustinian canons.

House of the Tailor of Gloucester

9 College Court
☎ 01452 422856
The little shop where Beatrix Potter set her story about the Tailor of Gloucester, Simpkin the Cat and the mice.

Gloucester Folk Museum

99–103 Westgate Street GL1 2PG
☎ 01452 396868
Tudor buildings and extensions illustrating social history, crafts, trades & industries of Gloucester from 1500 to the present. Interactive gallery, garden, cafe and shop.

Gloucester City Museum & Art Gallery

Brunswick Road GL1 1HP
☎ 01452 396131
History of the county with prehistoric and Roman remains, decorative arts, furniture, ceramics and paintings.

Robinswood Hill Country Park & Rare Breeds Centre

Reservoir Road GL4 6SX
☎ 01452 303206
250 acres (100 hectares) of Cotswold countryside with extensive views. Footpaths, nature trails, rare breeds centre.

National Waterways Museum

Gloucester Docks GL1 2EH
☎ 01452 318200
Installed in a Victorian warehouse the History of Britain's inland waterways. Interactive displays, touch-screen computers, working models, archive film and historic boats illustrate canal life and work.

Eastgate Viewing Chamber

Eastgate Street
☎ 01452 396131
Remains of the City's East Gate, dating from Roman times and lasting into the 17th century.

Blackfriars Priory

Ladybellegate Sreet
☎ 01452 396572
One of the most complete surviving English Dominican friaries, later converted to a Tudor house and cloth factory. Notable features include a fine scissor-braced dormitory roof and the oldest surviving purpose-built library in Great Britain.

Gloucester Antiques Centre

1 Severn Road, Gloucester Docks
☎ 01452 529716
140 dealers in antiques and collect–
ables housed in a huge Victorian
grain warehouse in the Docks.
Cafe.

Soldiers of Gloucestershire Museum

Gloucester Docks GL1 2HE
☎ 01452 522682
Military history of Gloucestershire
over 300 years.

St James's City Farm

23 Albany Street
☎ 01452 305728
Inner city farm providing hands-on
contact with farm animals. Rare
breeds of pigs, sheep, goats and
poultry. Outdoor picnic site.

The Wharf House

At Over, on NW outskirts of city
GL2 8DB
☎ 01452 332900
Exploring 750 years of the Leadon
Valley from the Civil War, basketry
& willow growing to the ongoing
restoration of the Herefordshire &
Gloucestershire Canal.

Nature In Art

Wallsworth Hall, Twigworth
GL2 9PA
☎ 01452 731422
Art gallery dedicated exclusively to
art inspired by nature. Collection
includes work from 60 countries,
spanning 1,500 years by over 600
artists and craftspeople. Gardens
and sculptures, children's play area
and activities, cafe.

THE SEVERN VALE

St Augustine's Farm

At Arlingham, 1 mile (2km) NW of
Frampton-on-Severn
☎ 01452 740277
Dairy farm with hands-on activities for
children. Woodland trail, playground,
cafe.

Wildfowl and Wetlands Centre

At Slimbridge, 12 miles (20km) SW
of Gloucester off A38
☎ 01453 891900
World-famous centre for wildfowl
conservation. Award-winning visitor
centre, wildlife art gallery and
observation towers surrounded by
thousands of ducks, swans and
geese.

Berkeley Castle

16 miles (25km) SW of Gloucester
on A38
☎ 01453 810332
Extensive remains include original
keep, 14th-century Great Hall,
staterooms with fine furnishings and
decorations, Edward II's dungeon.
Programme of special events.

Edward Jenner Museum

Church Lane, Berkeley
☎ 01453 810631
Commemorates discoverer of smallpox vaccination in the house he provided for his first 'guinea pig'.

5. Leamington Spa, Kenilworth and Warwick

We begin our exploration of the Avon with three Warwickshire towns which, despite their close proximity, have highly individual characters that prevent their becoming a conurbation.

Leamington Spa is the youngest. Its name has become a symbol of upper-middle-class respectability, so it comes as a surprise to find a busy commercial and manufacturing centre with a cosmopolitan population. Extensive recent development, however, has done nothing to erase the town's personality, exemplified in a spacious layout, elegant terraces and squares, wide streets, leafy avenues and dignified architecture.

Leamington was a late but quick developer. In 1800 it was a village with little more than 300 inhabitants. One or two of the saline springs that were to make its fortune had been discovered

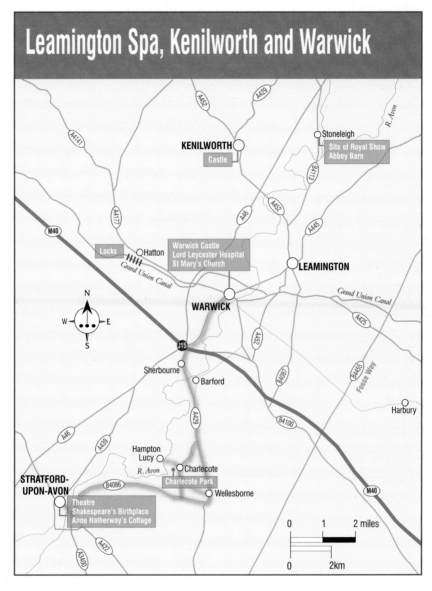

Leamington Spa, Kenilworth and Warwick

KENILWORTH
Castle

Stoneleigh
Site of Royal Show
Abbey Barn

R. Avon

M40

Locks

Hatton

Grand Union Canal

Warwick Castle
Lord Leycester Hospital
St Mary's Church

LEAMINGTON

Grand Union Canal

A425

WARWICK

Fosse Way

J15

Sherbourne

Barford

Harbury

A429

Hampton
Lucy

R. Avon

Charlecote

**STRATFORD-
UPON-AVON**

Charlecote Park

Wellesborne

M40

Theatre
Shakespeare's Birthplace
Anne Hatherway's Cottage

| 0 | 1 | 2 miles |

| 0 | 2km |

in the 1780s, notably by Benjamin Satchwell, who was the first to publicise them. In 1814 Henry Jephson, a local doctor, opened the Pump Rooms next to the River Leam, offering curative treatments. It was the charisma of Jephson that attracted aristocratic patronage in the early nineteenth century, and the town's reputation was enhanced by the conferring of royal status by Queen Victoria.

When the spa cult faded, Leamington retained its vitality by being adaptable. It was already a fashionable shopping centre, but industrial development in post-war Coventry brought other opportunities, including ancillary factories and a big influx of commuters.

A walk around Leamington Spa

The **Pump Room** beside the River Leam is an appropriate place to start a walk. It is not the imposing building you might expect, but its present clean-cut facade with a fine colonnade is deceptive. The design seems to be classical Regency, but photographs from the 1950s show it with an ungainly tower at one corner and a multitude of embellishments at roof level. These were added in 1862, and their subsequent removal must be counted an improvement. The modest front conceals quite a large complex, including the library, the museum and art gallery and a restaurant.

Its most prominent neighbour is the **church of All Saints**, one of Britain's largest and most impressive parish churches. The site was originally occupied by a twelfth-century chapel of ease, but the rapidly growing town demanded something grander, and in 1843 the Revd John Craig inaugurated the building of this massive example of Victorian Gothic. It took a long time to complete, and the final stage, the tower, was not added until the turn of the century. It follows that the church contains nothing of great historical interest, but the Anglo-Catholic tradition of worship has resulted in a most sumptuous interior, the outstanding feature being a magnificent rose window in the south transept. Having said that, it may come as a surprise to find the west end fitted out as a cafe.

Return over the bridge and through the gates between the two small lodges opposite the Pump Room. This is the entrance to one of Leamington's greatest assets, the **Jephson Gardens**. There was a public open space here in 1836, but as a tribute to Henry Jephson additional land was acquired from the Willes family and the present gardens were established in 1848. They contain just about everything one could wish for in a park – lawns, flowerbeds, fine trees, a lake with fountains, a pavilion for tea and the river running by. They are heavily used but manage to keep their air of Victorian distinction.

It is possible to leave the gardens at the far end, at Willes Road, where a left turn brings you to **Lansdowne Circus**, a tight circle of delightful small houses of 1835. Nathaniel Hawthorne, the American writer, lived here for a time at No. 10, and his own description still conveys the character of the Circus: 'One of the cosiest nooks in England . . . a circular range of pretty, moderate-sized, two-storied houses, all built on nearly the same plan and each provided with a little grass plot, its flowers, its tufts of box framed into cubes and other fantastic shapes, and its verdant hedges shutting the house in from the common drive and dividing it from its equally cosy neighbours.'

The little enclave is tucked away at one end of **Lansdowne Crescent**, one of Leamington's best Regency terraces. From here continue straight along Warwick Street to the **Parade**. From this point there is an excellent view of what is probably the most handsome shopping street in the Midlands. It was designed to impress and it still does, with an immensely long sweep of dignified frontages sloping down almost to the Pump Room. At the top of the Parade turn left and walk along to **Clarendon Square**, another of the town's showpieces. Expansive in design and built around a large central garden, it has considerable architectural variety. The west side was obviously intended to be superior, judging by the private drive, the screen of trees and the very fine ironwork. The notorious Aleister Crowley, dabbler in the occult, was born at No. 30 Clarendon Square and Napoleon III spent some time at No. 6 while in exile.

There is more impressive architecture in Clarendon Place, which leads downhill from the south-west corner of the Square along the western edge of Leamington's grid layout. Cross Warwick Street and turn left into **Regent Street**, which is a more humdrum commercial thoroughfare with an interesting mixture of smaller buildings. At its junction with the Parade, turn right. Dominating the

opposite side of the Parade are the **Regent Hotel** and the **Town Hall**, each in its own way symbolising the spa's past grandeur. The Regent opened in 1819 as the William Hotel and was the largest hotel in England at the time. Very soon afterwards the Prince Regent visited the town and was sufficiently impressed to give the hotel its present name. It now serves rather less exaltedly as a Travelodge. Its elegant symmetry is in striking contrast to the eccentricity of its neighbour. In fact it is difficult to know what to say about this late Victorian extravaganza, which appears to have been designed by assembling in random order all the illustrations from a history of architecture. However, the Town Hall is an endearing building, and Leamington can easily tolerate this kind of outrageous individuality.

At the lower side of the Town Hall, **Regent Grove** defies the grid plan by leaving the Parade at an angle. It was created in 1829 by the Willes family as a carriage drive from the town centre to their mansion at Newbold Comyn, just to the east of the town. It contains some exceptional Victorian houses and is a reminder that the Newbold Comyn estate is nowadays a public recreation centre.

The name occurs again a little further down, where the splendid **Newbold Terrace** runs alongside the Jephson Gardens. Some of its large Victorian villas can still be seen, and Newbold Street, which leads from it halfway along, is another example of Leamington's Regency style.

This walk will have revealed some of the attractions of the 'new' town centre that developed with Leamington's rapid recognition as a leading spa, but the original settlement was on the south side of the river behind All Saints' Church. Nothing now remains of the old village of **Leamington Priors**, but the earliest surviving buildings can be seen by crossing the bridge, turning left into Priory Terrace and then right into George Street and Mill Street. Satchwell Place dates from 1805, and the streets around it represent the very early development away from the original nucleus where the mineral springs were situated.

Effective landscaping has turned the modest **River Leam** into an asset. After running through the Jephson Gardens it continues west to join the Avon and provides a pleasant stroll by way of a bridge behind the Pump Room and a riverside walk that extends into Leamington's other main green space, **Victoria Park**. A more ambitious walk (marked on the OS map) begins at the entrance to **Newbold Comyn**, continues west across the former Willes estate for a mile, crosses the Leam and passes through the park of Offchurch Bury into the pleasant village of **Offchurch**.

On to Kenilworth

It is a quick drive to Kenilworth along the main A452 road, but a diversion through **Stoneleigh** provides a more interesting route. Shortly after leaving Leamington on the A452 turn onto the B4113 for about three miles (5km). The **National Agricultural Centre** is situated here and once a year it is the scene of the massive Royal Show, but it also stages events at other times

and it is worth enquiring about the programme.

The showground is part of the **Stoneleigh Abbey** estate. A disastrous fire in 1960 destroyed much of this celebrated house, but the owner, Lord Leigh, set out determinedly to restore it. In 1996 ownership passed to a charitable trust, and now the riverside gardens and many rooms in the house are open to the public. The first buildings here were part of a twelfth-century monastery, although only the gatehouse and an undercroft (now a restaurant) remain from this period. The present house is part Elizabethan and part eighteenth-century. Some fine plasterwork and panelling survived the fire, and other outstanding features are the staircase, the Saloon, the library and the exquisitely decorated bedroom used by Queen Victoria in 1858.

Stoneleigh itself was no doubt once a lively and bustling estate village, but the cottages have now become prim and immaculate under new ownership. They exemplify a range of styles – brick, timber, thatch and at least one cruck cottage opposite the post office. **St Mary's Church**, though, is a gem. The exterior shows Norman traces, including an interesting tympanum over the north door, and the interior is dominated by what must surely be the finest Norman chancel arch in the county. Apart from the elaborate carving on the arch itself the piers are finely decorated and have some homely individual touches. The chancel contains a huge black and white marble monument to Duchess Dudley, who died in 1688, and there is a sandstone memorial to an anonymous priest.

The Pump Room columns Leamington Spa

Kenilworth Castle, the wing built by Robert Dudley for Elizabeth I (below left)

The gatehouse (below right)

The font, bearing carvings of the twelve apostles, is Norman and the church fittings are completed by some exceptional early nineteenth-century woodwork.

Kenilworth

Approaching from this southerly direction you enter the town through the shopping centre that looks like any suburban High Street, and the modern development of Kenilworth is neatly symbolised at the top, where a Victorian clock tower is incongruously dwarfed by the huge De Montfort Hotel behind it. Turn left here and follow the signs to the **castle**, where there is a large car park.

The extensive ruins in warm red stone are the result of action by Oliver Cromwell's men, who held it after the Battle of Edgehill and did their best to render it useless when they left it. Building started in the twelfth century, and the original keep survives, but as usual the castle was modified and extended with notable additions by John of Gaunt. It figured largely in Simon de Montfort's rebellion against Henry III; de Montfort had acquired it on marrying Henry's sister, and following his death at the battle of Evesham in 1265 his son garrisoned the castle against the royal forces, enduring a six-month siege before surrendering. It remained in royal possession until 1563, when Elizabeth gave it to her favourite Robert Dudley, who entertained her lavishly there in 1575.

Visitors enter along a causeway that once crossed a lake. It partly encircled the castle to the south and was one of its most formidable defences. The Parliamentarians deliberately destroyed the dam that created it, and now the lake bed to right and left of the causeway is used as pasture. A detailed guide to the castle is available, and indeed is essential to understand the complex ruins that include the Keep, John of Gaunt's banqueting hall and some of Dudley's additions, in particular the fine four-storey gatehouse.

Old Kenilworth is separated from the new development by **Abbey Fields** to the east of the castle, and it is possible to walk through them to reach **St Nicholas's Church**, which had a substantial Victorian restoration that left little of great interest apart from the fine Norman west doorway. Close by are the ruins of Kenilworth Abbey, founded in 1122 and now virtually reduced to its foundations. The **Abbey Barn** contains good examples of the stonework as well as other archaeological finds and some agricultural exhibits. Also worth visiting are **Little Virginia**, a group of cottages at the east end of the High Street (traditionally the site of the first planting of Raleigh's Virginia potatoes) and **Castle Green**, a well-restored row of small houses just outside the castle walls to the east.

On to Warwick

Leave Kenilworth on the A452, then take the A46 and branch off for **Warwick** town centre after about three miles (5km). Once in the town you are strongly recommended to follow the signs for Banbury, cross the junction at the castle gates and turn left immediately afterwards into **St Nicholas**

Park, just before the river bridge. This is not only a pleasant place to leave the car, but also a good starting point for an exploration of the town.

A walk around Warwick

It seems odd to begin in a suburb, but few tourists bother to walk round **Bridge End**, one of Warwick's most charming quarters. It is reached by crossing the river bridge (there is a famous view of the castle from here) and turning right. With its mixture of black and white and old brick cottages, and its tranquil air, Bridge End can rival any Warwickshire village. Return over the bridge, walk up to the castle gates and down the road just to the left of them. This is **Mill Street**, and its profusion of timber-framed houses with the castle looming above gives some idea of what Warwick must once have looked like.

One of the crucial events in the town's history was a disastrous fire in 1694 which changed the whole character of the centre. The Saxon settlement here was created by the daughter of King Alfred, and the town developed steadily with the building of a castle in 1086 and the later influence of the powerful Beauchamp family. But the fire swept away most of the huddled medieval buildings, and apart from the occasional survival, as here in Mill Street, most buildings in Warwick are of stone, or at least stone-faced.

In recent years the **castle** has become the centrepiece for visitors to Warwick. It has had an eventful history. Apart from the motte, there are few traces now of the Norman castle of the mid-eleventh century, and the present buildings date substantially from the fourteenth century when the Earldom of Warwick passed to the Beauchamps. Their sophisticated work was completed by the five-storey Guy's Tower of 1395. Following the rebellion and defeat of Richard Neville (Warwick the Kingmaker), ownership passed to the Crown, and Elizabeth later gave it to Ambrose Dudley, brother of Robert Dudley who received Kenilworth Castle. Up to this time the castle had been primarily a military fortress, but when it came into the possession of Lord Brooke in 1604 work began on converting it into a stately home, and apart from an interruption during the Civil War this process has continued. In 1978 it was sold to the Tussauds Group, who set about turning it into a more calculated tourist attraction.

There have been two main results: the development of ancillary attractions such as picnic areas, a children's playground, a woodland walk and medieval banquets, and a more theatrical approach to the buildings themselves. Thus in the state apartments you can now see a reconstruction of a Victorian house party complete with waxwork figures. It is all quite seemly and entertaining despite what the purists may say.

From the gates walk along Castle Lane and then along Castle Street into Jury Street. This is the eastern end of Warwick's main thoroughfare, and it shows off very well the town's Georgian and Victorian architecture. Continue towards High Street and the **Westgate**. There is much to admire on both sides

113

Warwick Castle opposite and above

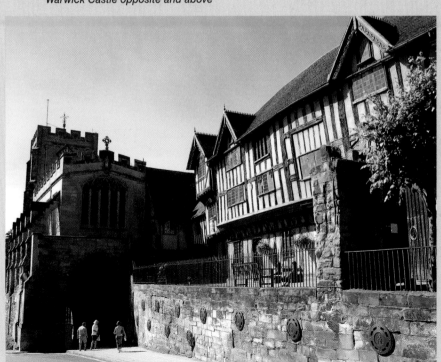

Lord Leycester Hospital founded by Robert Dudley

of the street, but Albion House and the Lord Leycester Hotel are outstanding. Westgate is the site of a very fine group of timber-framed buildings that escaped the fire and now press in on each side of the narrow gate.

Dominating the scene is the famous **Lord Leycester Hospital**, its irregular structure beautifully restored to something approaching authenticity. It was founded by Robert Dudley (later Earl of Leicester) as a place of retirement for old soldiers in 1571, but before that the buildings had served as the headquarters of three town Guilds, and also for a short time as the grammar school. Visitors can walk round the attractive courtyard and see some of the main rooms, including the Great Hall where James I was entertained, the Guildhall and the regimental museum of the Queen's Own Hussars, which is housed in the former Chaplain's Dining Hall.

If you now walk through the Westgate and turn right, a pleasant group of buildings, including a distinctive Victorian school, can be seen. Continue up Market Street and into the marketplace, where the former **Market Hall** is islanded. It is now the county museum. Prominent at the other end of the square is the new Shire Hall; it has incorporated some good earlier buildings, notably a fine town house called Abbotsford (at the corner of the Square) and an eighteenth-century house at the back of Northgate Street. It is worth walking to the top of Northgate Street to see Northgate House, which dates from 1698 and is a curious example of early semi-detached design with a central carriage gate.

St Mary's Church lies at the bottom of Northgate Street. It is one of the great sights of Warwick, not so much because of its exterior (the nave and tower were rebuilt after the fire) but because so much of value has survived inside.

The original collegiate foundation was established here in 1123, but only the crypt remains of the first Norman work. The other pre-eighteenth century portions are the fourteenth-century choir and the Beauchamp Chapel, which was started in 1442 and took many years to complete.

The pinnacled tower, 170 feet (52m) high, was splayed across the pavement as a way of securing a firmer foundation. Advice on this matter was given by one of Sir Christopher Wren's assistants, but there is no truth in the widely held belief that Wren himself designed the tower for a small fee. The nave is not particularly remarkable, apart from Thomas Swarbrick's fine organ case and the bread shelves on the south side from which loaves were given to the poor as a benefit of a local charity, but the lofty choir is magnificent, if rather dark at first appearance. Some ancillary buildings at the east end also survived the fire – a vestry, a vault where holy relics were once stored, and a chapter house.

The tomb in front of the high altar is that of Thomas Beauchamp, who commanded the English army at the Battle of Crecy and died of the plague in 1369. He and his wife lie in effigy with their hands linked. His grandson Richard has a far more elaborate memorial in the **Beauchamp Chapel**, which is the church's particular glory.

No expense was spared to produce a worthy tribute to this hero of the

Hundred Years War after his death in 1439; the finely detailed effigy in gilded bronze lies on a marble slab, protected by a framework of hoops, also gilded. The tomb is rightly the centrepiece of the chapel, although there are other monuments. Ambrose, the least distinguished of the Dudleys, lies nearby, while Robert, Earl of Leicester, has a characteristically huge and vulgar memorial totally out of keeping with the medieval surroundings which have been restored with splendid effect.

A walk down Church Street into Jury Street provides another chance to look at the handsome main street, and in particular at the **Courthouse**, built in the 1720s as a meeting place for the Corporation. Its best feature is the ballroom on the first floor, once the social centre of the town. Turn left towards Eastgate, which nowadays forces the traffic to go round it. The **Oken Almshouses** face the busy junction to the right of the gate, and the big house immediately beyond it on the left was the birthplace of the poet Walter Savage Landor.

Smith Street, lined with pleasant small shops, leads down from Eastgate to a road junction, and a little further on **St John's House** stands back on the right. With free admission this is one of the best bargains Warwick has to offer. In itself it is a handsome building of the Jacobean period, but it also houses two very interesting museums: on the ground floor is an imaginative display of costume and social history exhibits while the first floor contains the museum of the Royal Regiment of Fusiliers, into which the Royal Warwickshire Regiment was incorporated. It has a superb collection of medals and

fascinating mementoes of Lord Montgomery, the Royal Warwicks' most illustrious member.

The walk back to the starting point is by way of St Nicholas Church Street, which has its own mixture of interesting architecture. It may not be possible to get into the church itself, but it is an unusual example of a late eighteenth-century rebuild with an added Victorian chancel. St Nicholas Park is a good place to relax after a tour of the town since it provides not only rest and refreshment for weary adults but an excellent children's playground.

You can reach another good picnic spot by taking the A4177 out of town to the Grand Union Canal at Hatton, where the staircase of 21 locks is a scene of great activity in summer.

On to Stratford-upon-Avon

The A46 from Warwick to **Stratford** is a very dull road indeed, and the alternative A429 is infinitely preferable. It leaves the big motorway roundabout on the south-west outskirts of Warwick and at once invites a detour to **Sherbourne**, a secluded village with a mid-Victorian church that has elaborate carving round the door and statuary on the tower and north wall. It was paid for by a member of the Ryland family of Sherbourne House, who also provided the village's estate houses and school.

The next village is **Barford**, and its old centre is found by taking an unclassified road, formerly the B4462, on the left. The church is rather severe

Victorian but has some interesting features including a 'churching pew' at the back and a fourteenth-century effigy of a woman under the tower. Monuments to the Mills family in the chancel reveal that the Revd John was incumbent for 46 years and the Revd Francis for 50 years. Just beyond the church is the beautifully proportioned old vicarage (now Glebe House) and then a row of four highly individual cottages. In the first of these was born Barford's most distinguished son, **Joseph Arch**.

Joseph Arch of Barford

Arch's remarkable lifespan started in the reign of George IV and ended after World War I. His early years were spent as an agricultural worker, but his experience as a Methodist preacher gave him a talent for public speaking. In 1872 he addressed a large meeting at nearby Wellesbourne, thus inspiring the first steps towards the formation of a farmworkers' trade union. The immediate result was a major strike in south Warwickshire that ended successfully, and in May 1872 Arch became President of the National Agricultural Labourers' Union. In 1885 he was returned as the first farm worker to enter Parliament, but after this his militancy evaporated and he ended his life in comparative obscurity in the cottage in which he was born. His grave can be seen in the churchyard.

Back on the A429, two miles (3km) after Barford, a minor road branches right for **Charlecote**, the home for centuries of the Lucy family. There is a quite unfounded story that Shakespeare's departure for London was the result of his being caught poaching deer in the park here, and the legend has put the house firmly on the tourist map, although it needs no Shakespearean associations to make it an attraction. The visitors' car park is opposite the entrance, and the attractive setting of the house can be appreciated during the short walk through the deer park, which still supports a large herd. The building is often referred to as 'Tudor', but in fact the only surviving portion of the original 1550s house is the entrance porch; the remainder is the result of a discreet reconstruction in the early nineteenth century. The owner responsible for this was George Hammond Lucy, and it is his collector's taste that largely dominates the interior, which has been reconstructed to show the appearance of the principal rooms in mid-Victorian times. There is a wealth of pictures and furniture of fine pedigree, but the items that usually linger in the visitor's memory are the more eccentric pieces like a huge Venetian table, an ebony bed and the amazing sideboard in the dining room, constructed by Warwick craftsmen and intended as a present for Queen Victoria. The restored outbuildings, housing among other things a display of horse-drawn vehicles, complete an interesting visit.

The village associated with Charlecote is **Hampton Lucy**, reached by a lane that skirts the park and crosses the

Avon on a cast-iron bridge made in Shropshire. Many of the former estate cottages here were erected in the early nineteenth century, and at the same time the old **church** was demolished to make way for the present decorative building by Thomas Rickman. The impressive height of the exterior is matched inside, and the spacious effect is enhanced by the lack of obstruction between nave and chancel. The east end was completed by the addition of a graceful apse by Sir George Gilbert Scott in 1858. Intricately carved canopied stalls give richness to the chancel, and there is artistry too in the pews made of Charlecote elm. A charming old school building stands close to the church next to the less picturesque modern primary school.

A turning next to the Charlecote car park leads to **Wellesbourne**, which long ago outgrew its old nucleus (or rather nuclei because for centuries there was a settlement on each side of the River Dene). As you enter from the east there are signs of the old village around the church, which has an exceptionally good memorial brass to Sir Thomas le Straunge, while on the other side of the bridge is a village green with some attractive old houses and a memorial at the spot where Joseph Arch (see box above) addressed his historic meeting. Nearby is a restored working watermill open to visitors.

From here the B4086 takes you through the expensive eastern outskirts of Stratford, across the river and into the town.

Hatton locks

Places to Visit

IN AND AROUND LEAMINGTON SPA

Visitor Information

The Pump Rooms
☎ 01926 742762

Royal Pump Rooms

CV32 4AA
Leamington Art Gallery and Museum
Elegant assembly rooms, cafe.

Jephson Gardens

Beside River Leam, opposite Pump Rooms
Extensive and very attractive riverside gardens. Lake and tearoom. Named 'Best Park in England 2004'.

All Saints' Church

Imposing example of 19th-century Gothic style.

Town Hall

The Parade
Outstanding Victorian civic building in extravagant style.

Newbold Comyn

On eastern outskirts of town.
Former estate of Willes family. Good walking, golf and other sports facilities.

Leam Boat Centre

Mill Road
☎ 0845 456 9533
Wide range of craft for hire.

IN AND AROUND KENILWORTH

Tourist Information Centre

The Library, Smalley Place
☎ 01926 748900

The Castle

Extensive remains of original 12th-century keep with later alterations and additions, notably by John of Gaunt. Historical displays, tearoom. Home of Robert Dudley.

Abbey and Abbey Barn

Abbey Fields. Slight remains of abbey, but best of its stonework is preserved in Abbey Barn, together with various exhibits of local interest.

Stoneleigh Abbey

2 miles (3km) E of Kenilworth on B4115
☎ 01926 858535
18th-century house with earlier elements, including medieval undercroft and gatehouse. Fine staterooms with celebrated plasterwork. Landscaped grounds contain riverside gardens, walks and children's amusements.

Royal Showground

In grounds of Stoneleigh Abbey
Royal Show held here in early July, and also other events open to public.

IN AND AROUND WARWICK

St Mary's Church

Mainly rebuilt in early 18th century, but outstanding feature is magnificent 15th-century Beauchamp Chapel.

Warwick Castle

CV34 4QU

☎ 0870 442 2000

Claimed to be the finest medieval castle in England. Towers, dungeons, ramparts, state rooms (some with waxwork tableaux), Great Hall, etc. Extensive ancillary buildings and grounds with their own attractions.

Warwickshire Museum

Market Place, Warwick CV34 4NF

☎ 01926 412500

History of the county, geology, natural history.

St John's House Museum

Coten End CV34 4NF

☎ 01926 491653

Museum of Royal Regiment of Fusiliers (incorporating Royal Warwickshire Regiment). Also museum of social and domestic history, crafts etc.

Lord Leycester Hospital

High Street at West Gate

☎ 01926 491422

Impressive range of timber-framed buildings, established as retired soldiers' home in 1571. Chantry chapel, galleried courtyard, Great Hall, Guildhall. Regimental museum of Queen's Own Hussars.

Court House

Jury Street

☎ 01926 492212

Handsome building of 1720s with notable ballroom. Houses museum of the Warwickshire Yeomanry.

Priory Park

Children's adventure playground.

St Nicholas Park

Riverside gardens, swimming pool, children's amusements, etc.

Hill Close Victorian Gardens

☎ 01926 493339

Charming enclosed gardens created for 19th-century tradesmen.

Warwick Boats

☎ 01926 494743

St Nicholas Park. Wide range of craft for hire.

Funky Monkeys

Unit 1 and 2 Cape Road Industrial Estate

☎ 01926 409007

Elaborate children's play facilities. Cafe.

Hatton Locks

3 miles (5km) NW of Warwick

☎ 01926 409432

Flight of 21 Locks. Picnic area, canalside cafe.

Hatton Country World

3 miles (5km) NW of Warwick

☎ 01926 843411

Farm animals, demonstrations, adventure playground. Adjacent 'shopping village' features craft and gift shops, antiques, restaurant, etc. in Victorian farm buildings.

Heritage Motor Centre

Banbury Road, Gaydon CV350BJ

Off B4100 (M40 Junction 12), 12 miles (19km) SE of Warwick

☎ 01926 641188

World's largest collection of British cars. Cafe, museum, gift shop.

It has become customary to dismiss Stratford-upon-Avon as a tourist trap intent on selling trashy souvenirs to gullible visitors. Certainly it makes the most of its Shakespeare connections, but it is in fact a handsome market town that would attract visitors without the help of the bard.

If you come in from the north you will see the park-and-ride facility sign-posted, and in summer this is preferable to trying to park in the town, especially if you also use the tour buses that visit all the notable attractions.

A walk around Stratford-upon-Avon

The town centre is very compact and a tour is not hard on the feet. Start beside the river by the **Clopton Bridge**, the gift of Sir Hugh Clopton

Stratford-on-Avon and the Warwickshire Countryside

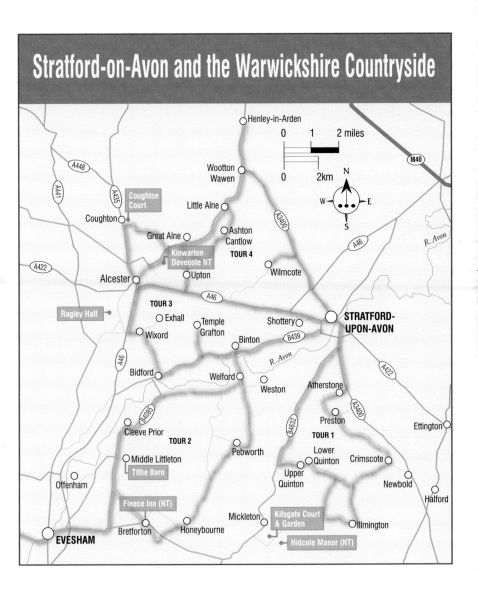

in the fifteenth century, which still carries traffic on its fourteen sandstone arches. Nearby is the old tramway bridge, now a footpath but once the trackbed of an early nineteenth-century horse tramway between Stratford and Shipston-on-Stour (one of its trucks has been preserved at the near end of the bridge). From here there is a famous view down the Avon, dominated by the Royal Shakespeare Theatre, with Holy Trinity church beyond.

Also nearby is the elaborate **Shakespeare Monument**, showing the playwright seated on a plinth and guarded by Hamlet, Lady Macbeth, Falstaff and Prince Hal. It is a remarkably lively piece of work created by Ronald Sutherland Gower in the late 1880s. This area was greatly enhanced in 1964 when the Stratford Canal was reopened after becoming derelict in Victorian times, and the terminus basin here is usually busy with holiday craft that add to the cheerful atmosphere of the riverside.

Walk up to **Waterside**, the street that runs parallel to the river. There are some interesting buildings in Waterside, especially the terrace of low cottages after the junction with Sheep Street, but the **Royal Shakespeare Theatre** is the main focus of attention here. The first Shakespeare Memorial Theatre was a rather intimidating Gothic structure erected in 1879; it was almost entirely destroyed by fire in 1926. Elizabeth Scott's new theatre, opened in 1932, caused much dismay at first with its uncompromising brick and severe lines, but its inviting frontage and the imaginative use of glass on the river side, together with its green setting,

made it a very acceptable feature of the townscape. At the time of writing in 2008 major structural alterations are under way to adapt the auditorium to modern requirements and to extend audience facilities, with the project scheduled for completion in 2010. In the interim, the Royal Shakespeare Company is continuing to present a varied programme of plays in other venues around the town.

Waterside becomes Southern Lane here. On the right the Black Swan now acknowledges on one side of its sign the nickname conferred by its actor customers over the years – the Dirty Duck. Turn left at the end of the lane and walk down to **Holy Trinity Church**.

The church is imposing – a reminder that well before Shakespeare's time Stratford enjoyed commercial prosperity as a market town and river port. The earliest foundation here in 1331 was a chantry chapel to Thomas à Becket, and Henry V authorised a collegiate church in 1415. The nave is high and fairly severe in style, and the eye is drawn at once to the intricate organ case at the tower crossing. In the north aisle the small Clopton Chapel contains some medieval glass and dignified monuments in subdued colours.

If you now wish to move into the chancel you may be asked for a 'donation'. The attraction, of course, is Shakespeare's tomb and the memorial bust. Their privileged position in the chancel was the result not of his literary reputation but his considerable wealth when he retired here from London. In fact neither tomb nor bust is particularly remarkable, but many visitors seem so transfixed that they fail to notice the fine windows or the misericords in the choir stalls. St Peter's Chapel to the south contains the unusual 'American Window', presented in 1896 by the American people and showing various figures from American history in a portrayal of the Adoration of the Magi.

After leaving the church turn left into **Old Town**. There are some fine buildings along here, particularly the Georgian Old Town Place and the Croft School on the left, but the most famous is **Hall's Croft**, the home of Dr John Hall, who married Shakespeare's daughter Susannah. It is a substantial three-gabled house, well restored by the Shakespeare Birthplace Trust, and the interior is furnished in Elizabethan and Jacobean style. The most intriguing feature is a re-creation of Hall's surgery, and visitors will also appreciate the immaculate garden.

At the top of Old Town turn right into **Church Street**, where there is also much to admire. **Mason's Croft**, on the left, was once the home of the novelist Marie Corelli, whose flamboyant behaviour enlivened and sometimes scandalised Stratford in the early years of the twentieth century. To the right is a magnificent range of fifteenth-century buildings comprising a group of almshouses and the original premises of the **King Edward VI Grammar School**, still an integral part of the modern school. Shakespeare was educated here, probably in the schoolroom on the first floor of the building that eventually took over the town's Guildhall. The Chapel of the Guild is next door. It was restored at the expense of Hugh Clopton and is notable for the

painting of the Last Judgement on the chancel arch.

Church Street becomes Chapel Street and the line of distinguished buildings continues with **Nash's House** on the right. It has an indirect connection with Shakespeare, in that Thomas Nash was the first husband of the playwright's granddaughter; more importantly it is the way in to New Place, the site of Shakespeare's own house during his retirement. It is now transformed into a charming Elizabethan garden. Nash's house itself contains a small museum relating to local history and there is a display of period furniture and household effects. On the other side of the road the Falcon Inn is a Tudor riot, but even more spectacular is the Shakespeare Hotel further along from Nash's House – it looks far too good to be true but most of it is authentic.

The wealth of timbering in Chapel Street throws the severe frontage of the **Town Hall** into sharp prominence. Constructed of Cotswold stone in 1767, it once accommodated an open cheese market at ground floor level, and on the first floor there is the customary ballroom designed as a meeting place for local society. At the crossroads with Sheep Street and Ely Street stands **Harvard House**, so named because it was occupied by the mother of John Harvard, whose bequest made possible the foundation of Harvard University. It now accommodates a museum of British pewter.

From the Town Hall you finally move into the High Street, where the shops begin to monopolise the town centre. The last house in the High Street belonged to Thomas Quiney, the husband

Outside the Courtyard Theatre, Stratford-upon-Avon

Canal boats, Stratford-upon-Avon

of Shakespeare's daughter Judith, and used to be the Judith Shakespeare Tea Rooms, fondly remembered by so many who came to Stratford on school visits.

To get to **Shakespeare's Birthplace** (isolated from the other famous buildings in the town) it is necessary to cross the road and walk up Henley Street. It is a workaday sort of road, and when you reach the celebrated house it turns out to be the least glamorous of the Shakespeare properties; a model, in fact, of plain and authentic restoration with no prettifying. An attempt has been made inside to recreate the atmosphere in which Shakespeare grew up and there are displays illustrating his career.

The short way back to the riverside and the car park is by way of Bridge Street, the broad and busy road that is bedecked during the summer with the world's flags. It has no famous buildings but its unstuffy, market-square atmosphere can come as a relief after the intense pursuit of history.

Exploring the Warwickshire countryside

Stratford is an excellent centre for touring some of the most attractive areas of Warwickshire, and the itineraries that follow include many of the small villages and market towns that give the county its character.

Tour 1: South of Stratford-upon-Avon

The first tour takes in the area south of Stratford. Leave Stratford on the A3400 and turn right after three miles (5km) for Atherstone-on-Stour. Almost at once the lane crosses the River Stour and the village is a short distance beyond. It is not much more than a small cluster of brick buildings and a farm, but the old centre is marked by the remains of a green and a huge, shapely chestnut tree, together with the former church and a handsome old rectory beyond. In contrast to the commuterised country to the north this area has an unpolished 'working' air about it, an impression reinforced as you continue along the lane lined by unmanicured hedges with acres of cornfield beyond.

The lane turns through a sharp right angle and comes into **Preston on Stour**. This is an estate village, and one of the most attractive and least spoilt places in Warwickshire. On entering the village there is a timber-framed house leaning backwards in a novel manner, and then a fine village green where it is possible to park and climb up to the church. James West, a mid-eighteenth-century squire, was responsible for having the church rebuilt by the famous Woodward brothers of Chipping Camden, although later restoration removed some of its Georgian character. The nave has a good Elizabethan roof with gilded roses, and the chancel is entered under a painted arch and through wrought-iron gates. The notable monument of 1624 to Nicholas Kempe and his two wives has no connection with the parish; it was brought here by West from a demolished chapel in London, and the same applies to much of the stained glass, which was accumulated from several countries. Note the modern memorial on the north wall of the nave, consisting of a bronze crucifix set on ancient timber.

After leaving the church walk down the village street between the two rows of trim nineteenth-century estate cottages, and take the left turn towards the bottom which enables you to see the rest of the village, formed of unassuming houses in a mixture of styles.

A mile (1.5km) from Preston the hamlet of **Wimpstone** marks the start of an isolated road with views down to the left over the valley of the Stour. Just outside Wimpstone, Whitchurch Farm lies beside the road as a reminder that there was once a village of that name to the south; its disappearance explains the solitary church standing in the fields only a short distance from the large settlement of Alderminster on the other side of the river (the church can be reached by a footpath from the farm). **Alderminster** spreads itself far and wide in the distance. It was once just another estate village but because of its convenient position on the A3400 it has been heavily developed in recent years and not much will be missed by bypassing it. At Crimscote, follow the sign for **Newbold on Stour** and join the A3400 on its northern outskirts. It is a pleasant stopping place with a pub, a green and a variety of houses old and new.

At the southern edge of Newbold there is a right turn for **Ilmington**, three miles (5km) away. Ilmington stands at the hub of a number of minor roads and was obviously a place of some importance before the main roads passed it by. It is large but very compact because of its horseshoe shape, and its mellow stone is a first indication that this is the fringe of the Cotswold country. If it has a centre it is a little green opposite the Howard Arms, a pub with a fine, plain frontage. The church is further towards the top of the village and very rewarding to visit. Norman work shows in the tower and in the two interior arches, and an odd feature is the two transepts. The north is fourteenth-century and the south is an almost exact copy carried out (very deceptively) in Victorian times. It contains an unusual plaque showing a bear-baiting scene. Three miles (5km) to the west of the village are two notable gardens open to the public – Hidcote Manor Gardens and Kiftsgate Court Gardens.

The itinerary continues on country lanes north-west of Ilmington to the Quintons. **Lower Quinton** is now dominated by military housing, but if the village has lost its character, St Swithin's Church is still notable for a fine Norman south arcade, a fourteenth-century statue of the Virgin in the Lady Chapel, a Norman font and a wall-painting in the south aisle. The unique feature of the church is a set of heraldic windows by Geoffrey Webb which includes a random collection of insects, butterflies and birds. **Upper Quinton** seems much more remote, with a scattering of houses round an immense village green. Meon Hill, immediately to the south, reaches a modest 600 feet (190m), but in this flat landscape it is a real landmark. Not surprisingly there is an Iron Age camp on its summit, which can be reached on foot from Upper Quinton.

The return to Stratford is by way of the nearby B4642 through rather featureless countryside, but it is worth stopping on the way back to visit **Clifford Chambers**. It is off the main road to the right, and can easily escape notice, but if you turn into its long street you find the attractive old village centre at the far end. The road is closed off by the manor house – a much-restored red brick mansion – but a footpath to the left of its gates leads to a watermill and fish hatchery beside the Stour. There are two very authentic, unrestored thatched cottages by the manor gates and a half-timbered rectory. The plain church has a filled-in Norman doorway in the north wall and two good Elizabethan brasses in the chancel, but the outstanding work is a very handsome coloured wall monument to Sir Henry Rainsford and his wife, showing the couple with their three children beneath, the youngest looking very long-suffering in swaddling clothes. From here it is two miles (3km) back to Stratford.

Tour 2: Between Stratford and Evesham

The second tour explores the villages to the south-west. Once again the route lies through 'working' countryside and extends to the horticultural area east of Evesham. Leave Stratford by the B439 (Evesham) road and turn left after 3 miles (5km) to **Welford on Avon**, which stands in a big loop of the river. As you enter the village between modern houses and immaculately groomed gardens, it becomes clear

that development and over-restoration has done its worst here, and unless you want to stop and admire the lofty maypole it is best to pass through and take the lane on the left to **Weston**. Here there are some unpretentious thatched cottages and an excellent small church where the huge windows show off the interior to advantage. The ancient doors, the panelled nave and the two fine brasses in the sanctuary repay a visit.

Return to Welford and take the left turn to **Barton**. The road follows the Avon and there is the first hint of orchard country to the south of the village. Barton is a small place with a harmonious grouping of cottages near a pub with the unusual name of 'The Cottage of Content', and a footpath leads down to a lock and weir. Just beyond the village you join the B4085 and pass the outskirts of **Marlcliff**, another hamlet backing on to the river and worth turning off for. A mile or so further on is **Cleeve Prior**, the first village in Worcestershire and a place of considerable charm. It is possible to park just after the King's Arms and walk back to the entrance to the village to see the manor house. It may be thought that this is all there is to see, but Cleeve Prior is deceptively shaped, and by taking the footpath opposite the King's Arms and walking along the edge of the churchyard you arrive at the real centre flanked by the village hall and a row of attractive low cottages. The main street leads away from here and is a model of success in absorbing new buildings into an old setting.

After Cleeve Prior the road runs along a hill above the Avon. For some

Caughton Court (above & below)

Kinwarton Dovecote

Above & above right: Alcester

time now the surrounding land has had a distinctive market-garden look, for this is 'grower's country'. It is not beautiful (intensively cultivated land rarely is) but it is hard-working countryside and the preserve of the stoical group of people who opt for one of the most precarious ways of living off the land, constantly vulnerable to weather or political conditions.

The road bypasses North, Middle and South Littleton in quick succession. There is nothing picturesque about them, but one thing should certainly not be missed. Turn left into **Middle Littleton** and follow the lane down about half a mile (1km) to the church. At the back of it is an immense medieval tithe barn, dating from abut 1300 and still in use, although now in the ownership of the National Trust and open to the public. Measuring 136 feet (41m) long and 36 feet (11m) wide, it has massive roof timbers and two huge wagon porches.

Down by the river on the other side of the B4085 **Offenham** has become something of a resort for Midlanders, with a large caravan park, a popular pub and much fishing and boating activity. During the summer the scene is enhanced by the procession of holiday craft negotiating the lock.

With Evesham virtually in sight, this is the furthest point of the itinerary. The run back to Stratford starts on the minor road through Offenham Cross and Blackminster. After three miles (5km) it reaches **Bretforton**, a sprawling village these days but with a charming centre comprising a green, a manor house and **The Fleece**, which is believed to be the oldest pub in Worcestershire and is one of very few village inns owned by the National Trust. Its great pride is a set of pewter ware given by Cromwell in exchange for the equivalent in silver. The church has been heavily restored, but one of the columns in the nave has a thirteenth-century capital illustrating the legend of St Margaret of Antioch, who used a crucifix to prise open the jaws of a dragon that had swallowed her. In the south chapel there is an exquisitely carved medieval bench and the windows here have unusual landscaped scenes. The steps to the former rood loft have survived.

From the northern edge of Bretforton a lane leads to a place called **Honeybourne** on the map, although it is in fact two villages separated by the Roman Rykneld Street. Cow Honeybourne, to the west, is a nondescript place with a vestigial village green, and Church Honeybourne is equally undistinguished, although its church, isolated on the southern outskirts, has some interesting architectural details, including a quaint stone-roofed porch and a massive buttress propping up the tower.

Now pass under the railway and make for the more rewarding village of **Pebworth**, two miles (3km) away. The original centre is on a steep hill with the church occupying a commanding position. It has a fine medieval door and ironwork, but restoration has not left a great deal of interest apart from the remains of the rood-loft stairway and a very impressive eighteenth-century memorial to Robert Martin in the south aisle. Ranged about the church are large and small houses that have been restored in an unpretentious way. The three-storey New Pebworth House, its multi-gabled neighbour and the Knoll, a Jacobean house in the same row, are particularly handsome.

A rather lonely lane due north of Pebworth leads to **Dorsington**, and from there it is a short distance back to Welford and the main Stratford road.

Tour 3: West to Alcester and Coughton Court

The third tour, in contrast to the last excursion into the fruit and vegetable country, is through familiar War-wickshire landscape, green wooded and prosperous looking. It starts on the A46 (Alcester) road heading west; after a mile or so (c.1½km) turn left to find one of the world's most famous houses. **Anne Hathaway's Cottage** is in fact a fairly substantial farmhouse, and is one of the larger buildings in **Shottery**, which manages to retain the appearance of a village in spite of being almost engulfed by Stratford's housing developments. Shakespeare's marriage to Anne

Hathaway is shrouded in mystery, and we have no knowledge of what happened to her after her husband's departure for London, so it is interesting to discover that the descendants of her family occupied this house until 1892, when it was acquired by the Shake-speare Birthplace Trust. It is important as an authentic example of a yeoman's homestead, comparatively unaltered since the sixteenth century in spite of the chocolate-box quaintness inflicted on it, and its contents reflect its history and character.

After returning to the A46 you quickly join the A46, then travel through pleasant rolling countryside to **Alcester**. The main road bypasses the town centre and it is all too easy to overlook what is possibly the most attractive small town in the county. In Roman times it was a thriving market town, and its Roman heritage can be explored in a lively museum in Priory Road.

A walk around Alcester

The car park is in the High Street. It is best to begin by walking up to where the old **Town Hall** forms an island. It is basically of the seventeenth century, timber-framed above a stone-built ground floor which was originally open to provide space for a market. There are some distinguished buildings to admire in **Henley Street**, behind the Town Hall, and more in **Butter Street**, the tiny thoroughfare beside the church. The church itself was rebuilt in the eighteenth century after a fire, but its interior lacks the elegance usually as-sociated with the period, and the only really notable feature is the painted effigy of Sir Fulke Greville, the Lord of the Manor whose grandson became Earl of Warwick. Note the clock positioned on the angle of the tower, presumably to make it visible from the High Street, which stretches away handsomely from the church door. Before starting to walk down it, cross Church Street to see **Malt Mill Lane**, a most successful example of conser-vation. The narrow thoroughfare is lined with houses restored judiciously

Preston-on-Stour

Middle Littleton Tithe Barn

The Fleece Inn (above) and parish church at Bretforton

to give a unified impression of a medieval street.

The **High Street**, like so many in the small towns of the Midlands, is a harmonious blend of styles with Georgian predominating. It is a pleasure to look at the countless interesting details of the facades. Bowen's, on the left, has very unusual sash windows, but the most elegant premises are those at the bottom of the street. Here is a solid Georgian building that houses Lloyds Bank. **Leachfield Road** runs along the side of the bank and as fine a row of modest houses as you will see anywhere, especially the former artisans' cottages towards the end. Considering the enormous development that Alcester has seen in recent years it is remarkable that its centre should remain so unspoilt while still serving its purpose as a very practical commercial area.

One or two interesting short trips can be made from here. A mile to the south-west of the town is **Ragley Hall**, the home of the Marquess of Hertford and well established as one of the major stately homes open to the public. Less well known is **Coughton Court (National Trust)**, two miles (3km) to the north on the A435. For centuries it was the home of the distinguished Throckmortons, who were originally a Worcestershire family (from the village of Throckmorton near Evesham) and who acquired Coughton Court by marriage in 1409. They are remembered mainly for their staunch Catholicism, but they touched English history at many points after the Reformation. A Throckmorton girl became the secret bride of Sir Walter Raleigh, and there was a Throckmorton plot

against Elizabeth in 1583. During the conspiracy that became known as the Gunpowder Plot the wives of some of those involved took refuge at Coughton to await the outcome.

The centrepiece of the Court is the magnificent Tudor gatehouse, and there are buildings of the same period at the back of the house. The remainder suffered damage first during the Civil War and later in 1688 when the Court was attacked by an anti-Catholic mob from Alcester. As a result, the wings on each side of the gatehouse are in plain Georgian style. In the house are displayed three items of particular interest: a cape embroidered by Catherine of Aragon; the chemise worn by Mary Queen of Scots on her execution; and the abdication letter of Edward VIII. Two churches stand close to each other beside the house. St Peter's is Coughton's parish church, and is noted for its stained glass and some fine tombs (one stands in an unusual position in the middle of the nave). The other is the Roman Catholic church and is not normally open.

Just outside Alcester on the B4089 is a right turn into a lane leading to **Kinwarton**, and this makes a very pleasant excursion. It consists of little more than an old rectory, a farm and a tiny church with fourteenth-century glass in its windows. A famous dovecote (now owned by the National Trust) stands in the next field beyond the church. Also dating from the fourteenth century, it has 600 nesting boxes and the original access ladder inside a low, ogee-shaped door. It is possible to take a short walk from here beside the River Alne to **Hoo Mill**, which is recorded in the Domesday Book, although the present buildings are of the early nineteenth century.

Continuing the tour, leave Alcester on the A46 and almost immediately turn left onto a minor road for **Wixford**, a small place with the usual collection of restored cottages and a church (down a sunken lane to the north) renowned for possessing one of the finest memorial brasses in Britain. Nearly five feet (1.5m) in length, it commemorates Sir Thomas de Cruwe and his wife and dates from 1411. Note also the wall brass to Rice Griffyn who died '3/4 old' in 1597. Outside there is a celebrated yew tree and a thatched shed once used by the incumbent to stable his horse. On driving out of the village you pass the Three Horseshoes, a very picturesque seventeenth-century pub, and from here follow the signs to **Bidford-on-Avon**.

Most guidebooks dismiss Bidford as hopelessly spoilt, and if you go there during a hot weekend in summer you can see why – the riverbanks by the old bridge attract a throng of families enjoying themselves in and out of the water. Few people seem to venture away from the river, but by turning just before the bridge into the narrow High Street and parking opposite the church you will find a most attractive little town centre with small Georgian houses and shops and several older buildings. The High Street retains a good deal of character. The venerable building at the corner of Church Street and High Street was once the Falcon Inn, reputed to have been patronised by Shakespeare. St Lawrence's Church is spacious and dignified with a light nave and dim religious chancel, and at

its back the charming Grange Road leads away beside the river.

Return to the roundabout on the B439, take the Stratford road and turn left after half a mile (1km) for **Temple Grafton** and its neighbour **Ardens Grafton**. Their names make them sound snug and picturesque but surprisingly they turn out to be wind-swept hill villages with houses built of the limestone on which they stand. Ardens Grafton has a huddled air and is the more prettified of the two (there are exceptionally fine views to the north), while Temple Grafton retains more of the atmosphere of a working community.

Rejoin the Stratford road for just over a mile and turn left for **Binton**, where the church has a unique stained-glass window. In the early years of the century the rector was Lloyd Harvey Bruce, whose sister married the explorer Captain Scott. After the deaths of Scott and his companions in Antarctica a memorial window was installed at the west end of the church. It shows four episodes of the expedition, including Oates' famous 'walk'. Another interesting feature is the mounting block with tethering ring at the gate. Binton completes this itinerary.

Tour 4: North to Henley-in-Arden

The fourth tour explores the area to the north towards Henley-in-Arden. This is Birmingham commuter country, and there are very few places left unspoilt either by insensitive new housing, the over-restoration of old cottages or a combination of both. However, it is

Church, Wootton Wawen. The lower photograph shows the Saxon base of the tower

High Street, Henley-in-Arden

The village hall, Aston Cantlow

still possible to find features of interest, and the first stop is one of the more obvious. Leaving Stratford on the A3400 north, turn left after 2½ miles (4km) for **Wilmcote**. Mary Arden's House is on the right just after the railway and canal have been crossed.

Mary Arden was Shakespeare's mother, and her former home is a splendid Tudor farmhouse with elaborate timbering and a tiled roof. The house and the farm buildings behind it were in use until 1930. The Shakespeare Birthplace Trust have now restored some of the appearance and atmosphere of Mary Arden's day, installing some fine examples of country furniture and creating a small agricultural museum in the farm buildings. Until the early years of the twentieth century Wilmcote was a small settlement of quarry workers housed in rows of stone cottages – some are still visible though barely recognisable in many cases – and there was no church until the 1840s, when St Andrew's was built to embody the new ideas of the Oxford Movement regarding ritual and ornament. It is still a distinctive church, full of colour, with patterns and gilding in the chancel, illustrated texts on the walls, Stations of the Cross, sanctuary lamps and a very elaborate altar with a Tabernacle.

A further 3½ miles (5½ km) along the A3400 the road passes under a canal aqueduct and enters **Wootton Wawen** (pronounced 'Worn'), a village sliced in two by the widened main road. The River Alne runs parallel to the canal here, and drops over an impressive weir just beyond the aqueduct. The park on the right belongs to Wootton Hall, basically a seventeenth-century mansion

and once the home of Mrs Fitzherbert, mistress of George IV. In the centre of the village **St Peter's Church** stands on top of a rise with a green to separate it from the road.

St Peter's is one of Warwickshire's outstanding churches. Its castellated exterior gives it a late-medieval look, but the bottom of the tower is Saxon work, and the heart of the church is still the 'Saxon Sanctuary' formed by the tower base, with its four tenth-century arches and some good modern stained glass. A medieval wooden screen gives access to the chancel, which has a fine fourteenth-century east window. Members of the Harewell family are commemorated here by two brasses and an alabaster memorial, and there are some rare fifteenth-century pews that survived Victorian restoration. On the south side of the chancel is a huge Lady Chapel – a riot of memorials that repay close inspection. Another rare feature of the church is the chained library in the south aisle, given by a seventeenth-century incumbent.

From outside the church the surviving buildings of the old village can be seen, spread out below. The Bull's Head is a rambling pub that has been 'improved' out of all recognition, but there could well be an interesting timber-framed building behind all the cheap embellishment. The same fate has overtaken most of the old cottages; carriage lanterns and imitation bow windows abound. There is a welcome touch of individuality in the red-brick house opposite the church, topped with an incongruous thatched roof, and a good deal to be said for the Seymour almshouses next door, which have been built in sympathetic contemporary style and can claim to be the most pleasing buildings in the village.

Luckily nothing has been able to spoil the long sweep of the main street at **Henley-in-Arden**, two miles (3km) further on. In style it is like Alcester on a larger scale, although less fortunate in that the main street is a busy trunk road. It would be easy to spend an hour here simply admiring the endless variety of the facades, many of them concealing much older buildings. The natural centre of the town is at the Guildhall halfway up the High Street, and there are some handsome buildings here. Severe restoration has left the church of St John the Baptist with little to show, but there is compensation if you walk a few hundred yards behind it and across the river. Standing on its own, in surroundings that are suddenly rural, is the church of St Nicholas, where the superb Norman south door is matched inside by a dramatic chancel arch and small east window of the same period. The primitive air of this small church is most appealing. The hill behind it (accessible from the church) is the site of a Norman castle of which nothing now remains.

Return now to Wootton Wawen and turn right at the Bull's Head onto the B4089. After two miles (3km) take the lane on the left to **Aston Cantlow**, a village with strong Shakespearean connections – John Shakespeare married Mary Arden here in 1557. The name derives from the de Cantelupe family, one of whom was successively parish priest, Bishop of Hereford, Chancellor of England and St Thomas de Cantelupe. There is much modern housing before reaching the village centre, which is noted for one of the country's most distinguished parish halls, the timber-framed Guildhall that was restored through the efforts of the residents. The nearby King's Head, and some of the surrounding buildings, are of the seventeenth century. Another fine piece of restoration is Glebe Farm at the south end of the village street where there is a right turn to rejoin the B4089.

It is a short distance to **Great Alne**, now a rather shapeless village with at least one surprise. It is the former railway station, a flamboyant building now converted into a residence with its original exterior features virtually intact. The church at Great Alne is a Victorian rebuild of a nondescript kind, but one other feature of interest here is the restored watermill to the south, reached by a lane from the centre of the village.

Leave Great Alne on the B4089 Alcester road, and after a mile (1½km) turn left onto the minor road to **Haselor**, which is a rather confusing place apparently consisting of two hamlets called Upton and Walcot, which share a church situated between them. Parishioners experience a real test here because not only is the church on top of a hill, but access is only possible by foot. Both hamlets are worth looking at for the variety in their old buildings.

The lane that passes through Upton leads to the B46 and the return to Stratford, although after about two miles (3km), a left turn leads to the remaining traces of the deserted medieval village of **Billesley** to the south and east of the church (a leaflet is normally available in Wilmcote church).

Butter Street, Alcester

Places to Visit

STRATFORD-UPON-AVON

Visitor Centre

In Bridgefoot
☎ 0870 160 7930

The Shakespeare Properties

(All enquiries ☎ 01789 204016)
A tour bus stops at all the Shakespeare houses plus other places of interest. This is a hop-on hop-off service, frequent in the summer, and is useful for visiting the country properties, where parking can be difficult. The ticket is valid for one day. Enquiries to ☎ 01789 412680.

Shakespeare's Birthplace

Henley Street. Exhibits illustrating Shakespeare's life and work and the history of the house.

Hall's Croft

Old Town
Fine 16th-century house of Shakespeare's son-in-law, with period furniture and re-creation of Dr Hall's dispensary. Attractive walled garden.

New Place and Nash's House

Chapel Street
New Place is an Elizabethan garden on the foundations of Shakespeare's last home. Nash's House next door houses exhibitions.

Anne Hathaway's Cottage

Shottery, 1 mile (1½km) W of Stratford
Interesting example of Tudor farmhouse that survived comparatively unaltered. Period furniture and bygones.

Mary Arden's House

Wilmcote CV37 9UN, 3 miles (5km) NW of Stratford
The home of Shakespeare's mother; a working farm well into the twentieth century and now a farm museum.

Harvard House

High Street CV37 6HB
☎ 01789 204016
House of 1596, home of mother of founder of Harvard University. Houses pewter museum, with children's interactive displays.

Holy Trinity Church

CV37 6BG
☎ 01789 266316
Architecturally distinguished, contains Clopton Chapel, tombs of Shakespeare, Anne Hathaway, Thomas Nash, Dr John Hall. Shakespeare's wall memorial.

Royal Shakespeare Theatre

Tickets ☎ 0844 800 1110. Long summer season of Shakespeare performances. At time of writing (2008) in the process of reconstruction and refurbishment, plays are staged in the temporary Courtyard Theatre.

Places to Visit

Shakespearience

Waterside Theatre

☎ 01789 290111

One-hour virtual reality presentation of Shakespeare's life, work and legacy.

Brass Rubbing Centre

☎ 01789 297671

Avonbank Gardens, behind theatre. Some famous Warwickshire brasses in replica.

Butterfly Farm

Tramway Walk, Swans Nest Lane

☎ 01789 299288

Hundreds of species in tropical environment.

Avon boat trips

Bancroft Cruisers, Bridgefoot ☎ 01789 269669 & Avon Boating,, Bancroft Gardens ☎ 01789 267073 operate cruise boats on the Avon. Trips last 30 to 45 minutes.

Stratford-upon-Avon Canal

Southern terminal is in Bancroft Gardens. Good walk along towpath.

Stratford Greenway

Milcote CV37 8JW

☎ 01827 872660

THE FOUR WARWICKSHIRE COUNTRYSIDE ITINERARIES

Charlecote Park (National Trust)

4 miles (6½km) E of Stratford on B4086

☎ 01789 470277

Original Elizabethan house largely rebuilt in early 19th century. Home of the Lucy family. Interesting pictures and furniture, kitchens and collection of carriages. Deer Park. Children's play area, shop and restaurant.

Compton Verney

CV35 9HZ

7 miles (11km) E of Stratford on B4086

☎ 01926 645500

Grade I listed Robert Adam house in 120-acre (50 hectares) grounds by Capability Brown. Notable art gallery.

Coughton Court (National Trust)

B49 5JA

2 miles (3km) N of Alcester on A435

☎ 01789 400777

Home of Throckmorton family from 1409. Splendid early 16th-century gatehouse. Fine furniture and pictures. Riverside walk, rose garden, special display on Gunpowder Plot.

Ragley Hall

B49 5NJ
8 miles (13km) W of Stratford at Alcester
☎ 01789 762090
Stately home, well developed as tourist attraction. Imposing late 17th-century house with notable furniture, porcelain and paintings, including major contemporary mural by Graham Rust. Grounds by Capability Brown contain 'adventure wood', maze and other attractions for children.

Hidcote Manor Garden (National Trust)

8 miles (13km) S of Stratford off B4632
☎ 01386 438333
Grounds contain a series of specialised gardens. Rare shrubs, herbaceous borders, old rose species.

Kiftsgate Court Gardens

8 miles (13km) S of Stratford off B4632
☎ 01386 438777
Magnificent setting with extensive views. Vast plant collection, noted for largest English rose. Water garden.

Redwings Rescue Centre

At Oxhill, 9 miles (15km) SE of Stratford off A422
☎ 0870 040 0033.
Rescued horses and donkeys. Displays, talks and demonstrations. Cafe and shop.

Roman Alcester

Priory Street, Alcester B49 5DZ
10 miles (16km) W of Stratford
☎ 01789 762216
Museum illustrating the town's Roman origins and legacy.

Wellesbourne Watermill

6 miles (10km) E of Stratford off B4086
☎ 01789 470237
Working mill with one of the country's largest wooden waterwheels.

St Peter's Church

Wootton Wawen. 10 miles (16km) NW of Stratford on A3400
Warwickshire's most interesting church, with substantial Saxon work and Lady Chapel packed with memorials.

Bungo's Barn

At Bidford-on-Avon, 7 miles (11km) W of Stratford on B439
☎ 01789 778899
Children's 'soft play' centre with other family entertainment.

Evesham

Certain place names evoke clear mental pictures. We all think we know what Grimsby, Cheltenham or Scunthorpe look like even if we have never visited them. Evesham comes into this category, thanks to jam-jar labels and childhood geography lessons, but anyone expecting a sleepy town full of blossom will be disappointed. The town is businesslike, not particularly pretty, and has a serious traffic problem, but it is nevertheless worth seeking out its interesting features.

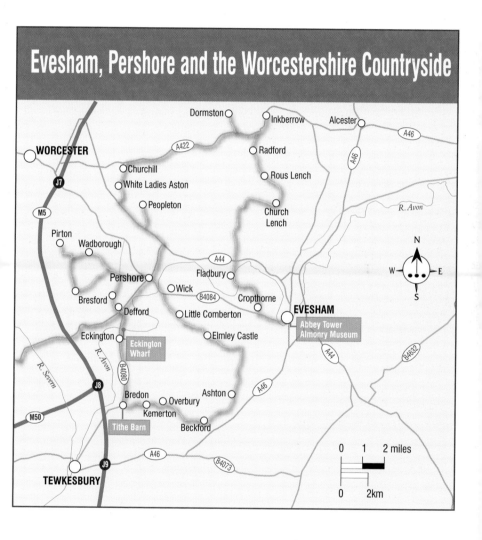

Evesham, Pershore and the Worcestershire Countryside

Dormston ○
Inkberrow ○
Alcester ○
A46

WORCESTER ○
A422
Radford ○

Churchill ○
Rous Lench ○
A46

White Ladies Aston ○
J7
M5
Peopleton ○
Church Lench

R. Avon

Pirton ○
Wadborough ○
A44
Fladbury ○

Pershore ○
Wick ○
Cropthorne ○
N
W ○ ● ● ● ○ E
S

Bresford ○
B4084
EVESHAM ●

Defford ○
Little Comberton ○
Abbey Tower
Almonry Museum

Eckington ○
Elmley Castle ○
B4632

Eckington Wharf
A44

R. Severn
R. Avon
B4080

J8
Bredon ○
Ashton ○
A46

M50
Overbury ○
Kemerton ○

Tithe Barn
Beckford ○

0   1   2 miles
A46
B4073
0   2km

TEWKESBURY
J9

A walk around Evesham

A good starting point is the **Bell Tower**, which stands on high ground above the river and is the principal landmark. It is one of the few remnants of an abbey which was once vast in size and possessions, and could boast of a foundation dating back to 714. Abbot Lichfield was responsible for adding the tower in the early sixteenth century, only a few years before the dissolution of the monasteries, and no doubt it was its new-built solidity that saved it from the fate of the other monastic buildings, which were demolished and used as a source of building stone. What survives is an elaborately decorated structure with ogee-shaped windows, ornamental castellation and much intricate carving.

From the foot of the tower there is a commanding view across the Avon. Evesham has made the most of its riverside land here, and the pleasant park and playground are a magnet for visitors in the summer, enjoying the holiday atmosphere of boats and water. The town lies on the opposite side of the tower through the former churchyard, where the sight of two substantial churches standing side by side may well cause some surprise. The explanation seems to be that St Lawrence's belonged to the abbey cemetery, and was later used for the benefit of the many pilgrims who flocked to this important foundation, while All Saints' was the parish church.

St Lawrence's, with the tower, is now redundant. It is the less interesting of the two, having been given a comprehensive and fairly dull restoration

during the 1830s. **All Saints'** also shows signs of Victorian attention, with a dark and heavy chancel behind a solid gated screen, but it has Norman work at the west end and a good chancel arch. The Chapel of Our Lady and St Egwin (c.1513) in the south transept commemorates Abbot Lichfield who is buried beneath it, and there is some fine fan vaulting.

By turning right outside the church door you pass into the town centre through the Norman cemetery gate and along a picturesque passageway. It leads into a square almost closed off on the left by the old **Town Hall**, Elizabethan in origin with eighteenth-century additions. It once had the customary arrangement of an open ground floor for market purposes, but its arches have been bricked up to provide draught-free accommodation. The medieval building that catches the eye straight ahead was formerly called the Booth Hall and is now known as the **Round House**, although it is demonstrably square. Although excessively restored it is a fortunate survival in view of Evesham's lack of major timber-framed buildings.

The Round House stands at the junction of three main streets. To the north is the **High Street**, a broad thoroughfare obviously intended to accommodate markets and fairs in the old days but now monopolised by buses and cars. The best buildings are on the left-hand side and range in age from the seventeenth to the twentieth century. **Dresden House** (1692) is outstanding; it acquired the name after an early owner, Dr William Baylies, became a physician to Frederick the Great of

Prussia and died at Dresden in 1787. Note also the **Star Hotel**, a handsome example of a Georgian inn.

To the east of the Round House is **Bridge Street**, a narrow shopping centre that also has some interesting frontages remaining at first-floor level. The oldest building here is probably the Crown Hotel, a rambling inn now much altered and restored.

Finally **Vine Street** leads away to the south, with some distinguished buildings facing the Town Hall. They include the half-timbered Royal Oak and the venerable Red Horse on the corner of Vine Street and Merstow Green. The latter is really another square, and if you walk down the right-hand side you pass the medieval former grammar school. It is worth continuing to the bottom to see some mellow cottages and the very pretty National Schools building of 1844, pink and mock-Elizabethan. Opposite the entrance to Merstow Green the **Almonry Heritage Centre** contains displays on local history and life. The half-timbered building with its rambling interior is a very successful restoration.

Exploring the Worcestershire countryside

Tour 1: Evesham to Pershore

From Evesham the Avon flows through giant meanders almost due west to Pershore. The countryside to the north of it is the heartland of Worcestershire,

and the itinerary that follows is designed to include the most interesting villages, but do not be too disappointed if there seem to be few signs of traditional village life. In recent years the area has been considerably gentrified with the result that the houses have been immaculately preserved but the old vitality of the villages has largely died. It is a pity that this reservation has to be made about so much of northern Worcestershire and Warwickshire, but it need not detract too much from the visual enjoyment of what is often regarded as quintessential rural England.

Leave Evesham on the B4084. The road passes through the suburb of Hampton, and 2m (3km) from the outskirts there is a lane on the right leading to **Cropthorne**. The sloping village street is lined with restored houses, brick and timber-framed, and the church is right at the top end. It is unusual in that the main interest lies in the nave rather than the chancel. On the south side is a ninth-century cross decorated with birds and animals, while the north arcade shows traces of wall painting. The pews are distinctively carved. The most prominent features, however, are two coloured tombs of the seventeenth century; one is a table tomb and commemorates Francis Dingley, who died in 1624, and the other, placed awkwardly askew against the chancel arch, dates from 1646 and shows the kneeling figures of Edward Dingley and his wife.

Fladbury lies a mile or so (c.1½km) across the Jubilee Bridge. There used to be a traditional rivalry between the two villages, but the impartial outsider will probably find Fladbury the more

149

The Round House, Evesham

The Norman Cemetery gate by All Saints Church. Evesham

All Saints (left); St Laurence's (middle) and the Bell Tower (behind right), Evesham

appealing. It has a spacious air, with the time-honoured nucleus of church, green and pub, and there seems to be a lot of activity. The extra liveliness may be due to some new housing that has been absorbed into the village with unusual success. There is a wide range of older buildings, humble and stately, with mellow brick predominating over black and white, and one magnificent Georgian house opposite the church. The best-known feature of Fladbury, however, is its mill, sympathetically restored as a private house and almost the first building passed as you enter from the south. Within living memory it provided the power to operate some of the first electric street lamps in any village in the country. The rather more functional buildings on the other side of the river are those of Cropthorne Mill.

The Throckmorton family (mentioned in Chapter 6 in connection with Coughton Court near Alcester) had their original home near Fladbury, and a family chantry was an early addition to the church, now a rather severe building with the neat and well-scrubbed look of Victorian restoration. The interest here is in embellishment rather than architecture; for example, the small fourteenth-century glass panel at the Lady Chapel altar. It shows the Virgin and Child, and a specially designed illuminated case allows you to appreciate the delicate colouring. There are some impressive memorials too; in particular the Throckmorton brasses on an altar tomb in the choir vestry, and two other fifteenth-century brasses, covered by carpets, on each side of the chancel. It is impossible to miss the marble monument of the Stuart period to Bishop William Lloyd that occupies the full height of a wall.

Continue through Fladbury, cross the A44 and take the next turning on the right for Church Lench. 'The Lenches' are a group of villages that must once have been very isolated, and even today they have a remote air, with hills on one side and orchards on the other. Of the group **Rous Lench** is possibly the most interesting. From this direction you enter it by driving down a steep hill, and the first building on the right is Rous Lench Court, which is not open to the public but which has a gate that can usually be peeped through unobtrusively for a view of the celebrated gardens and of the house itself, which is a curious mixture of styles and periods. The Court was the home of a remarkable Victorian squire and parson called Chafy, who ruled the village in a benevolent way between 1876 and 1916 and was responsible for refurbishing the church, thus ensuring its survival as one of the most remarkable in Worcestershire. The exterior looks entirely undistinguished apart from its small Norman door, but on stepping into the nave you find massive Norman pillars and a chancel arch of the same period. The staircase to the rood loft still remains, and there are two Elizabethan pulpits. On the north side of the chancel arch is a small mausoleum built by Dr Chafy and containing a variety of memorials removed here from elsewhere in the church. They include substantial effigies of Edward Rous and his wife (1611) and a rather quaint wall monument to Francis Rous, showing his wife sitting stolidly in a revealing dress and holding her heart. Another remarkable object here is a piece of carved stonework of Saxon origin. The church's biggest surprise, however, is the little Lady Chapel, Italian in style with a 'medieval' triptych, fluted columns, gold mosaic and an intricate altar canopy, all set within a miniature apse.

Rous Lench village is compact and charmingly set around a triangular green, with remains of a roofed well and probably the only half-timbered postbox in Britain. The unostentatious dwellings include a pretty converted school. It is all very dignified and contrasts strongly with **Inkberrow**, 3m (5km) to the north and reached by passing through Radford and joining the A422. There is a good deal of modern housing before reaching what is obviously the old village, where a lane to the right leads past the village green to the church.

Inkberrow is reputedly the model for Ambridge of *Archers* fame, and the Old Bull near the church does its best to live up to the image with much whimsical picturesqueness. The same applies to some of the other houses here, and the rash of new developments gives the place a suburban air that hardly justifies more than a brief stop.

Local literature describes some worthwhile walks around Inkberrow. Highly recommended is the short stroll on the bridleway to **Dormston**, where the church has been less restored than most and still has a timber-framed tower with a spectacular array of supporting struts and beams inside. The nave has leaning walls, traces of wall painting, venerable sixteenth-century pews and oil lamps. A rather longer walk from the

centre of Inkberrow takes you south-wards to the isolated village of **Abbots Morton**, while a third possibility is a walk to the attractive village of **Feckenham**, to the north of Inkberrow. Finally there is the **Wychavon Way**, a long-distance path that links most of the villages mentioned in the tour so far.

To the west of Inkberrow is a scattering of villages whose names could have been invented by PG Wodehouse – Upton Snodsbury, Flyford Flavell, Naunton Beauchamp, Broughton Hackett and North Piddle, to name only a few. They sound tempting, but being on or close to the main road they have become favourite dormitory villages and have largely lost their individual characters. Very little will be missed by driving quickly along the A422 (towards Worcester) and taking the left turn just after Broughton Hackett to **Churchill**.

It was at Churchill that a group of nuns of the Order of the Poor Clares were given shelter after fleeing from the French Revolution in 1792, and they are commemorated by a tomb in the churchyard. A mile (1½km) to the south, the straggling village of **White Ladies Aston** has some interesting houses and a church containing a memorial to a Victorian rector who served for the remarkable period of 71 years. Join the A44, and turn left after 2m (3km) to reach **Peopleton**, a cheerful village brightened by the colourful gardens of the former council houses that line the main road here, along with more expensive conversions. The church is a standard Victorian remodelling, but there is a charming individual touch in a chancel window that shows a

Above: Two interesting corners off The High Street, Evesham

The 'venerable' Red Horse pub in Vine Street, often plagued by traffic, Evesham

The Old School, Rous Lench

Inkberrow, the model for Ambridge in 'the Archers' radio programme

boy and girl unmistakably of the 1930s. From Peopleton it is a short distance to Pershore.

Pershore

This is a delightful place. The Avon loops round to the south and east but the town keeps a respectful distance from it; there is riverside activity here but none of the atmosphere of a riverside settlement. Broad Street, a square in everything but name, lies at the heart of the old town. At one end of it the long main street runs from north to south, its southern length a vista of harmonious and slightly aloof Georgian architecture and the northern stretch a concentration of commercial hustle and bustle. This rather class-conscious arrangement gives Pershore the advantage of having simultaneously a cheerful and convenient shopping centre and the most handsome and least spoilt main street in Worcestershire.

Nowadays the town is associated mainly with the fruit and vegetable trade, but the original settlement grew up around a tenth-century Benedictine monastery. By an obscure process, most of the land here was acquired at an early date by Westminster Abbey, which led among other things to the building of St Andrew's Church within a stone's throw of Pershore's own abbey. However, there are few relics of this early history in the streets now, and Pershore has a solid Georgian and Victorian character.

A walk around Pershore

A walk round the town is best started at its southern end, where the old bridge has become a pleasant picnic area. Walk up **Bridge Street** towards the town centre. There can be few towns where the principal thoroughfare begins so abruptly; the transition from riverside meadows to urban street is instantaneous. Every house in Bridge Street is worth studying, and there is room here only to pick out some of the outstanding features.

Almost immediately on the left two semi-detached houses with lattice balconies make a pleasant change from the usual Georgian town house, but the characteristic style soon reasserts itself with the imposing double frontage of Stanhope House on the right. A little further along the same side is an interesting juxtaposition of two more double-fronted houses, both numbered 31 but originally two separate dwellings, one definitely grander than the other. The pub almost next to them has a curious tower and doors and windows that give it an almost Moorish look. Then comes Perrot House, once the home of a judge and revealing a very superior taste. Of impressive dimensions, it is notable for its Venetian windows: the central one on the first floor is conventionally flat, but on the ground floor the design has been adapted for bay windows. The front door echoes the window shapes. Back on the left-hand side there is now an attractive range of small shopfronts, while opposite them Bedford House has canopied balconies of intricate ironwork.

You now reach **Broad Street** at a

corner monopolised by the former Three Tuns Hotel, with a sheer north wall relieved by wrought-iron balconies. The spacious effect of Broad Street is diminished nowadays by the ranks of parked cars, but it remains one of Pershore's best features, lined with small-scale shops and houses and closed off splendidly by a large house at the western end.

This is the way to the **Abbey**, which, with no disrespect intended, must be counted as something of an oddity. Although the monastic foundation was of pre-Conquest origin, the building that existed at the dissolution of the monasteries was largely of the thirteenth century. As at Malvern and Tewkesbury, the people of Pershore tried to purchase the Abbey but were rather less fortunate than their neighbours; they were too late to prevent the nave being demolished and were left with only the tower, the transepts and the choir. This still represents a good deal of space, but the loss of the nave means that the tower has had to be buttressed in rather unsightly fashion and the truncated exterior lacks graceful proportions.

On entering the west door, the visitor is bound to be impressed by the superb arcades and vaulting, but will also notice the lack of an opulent east window. The Victorian love of a dim religious light in the sanctuary led to the building of a rather pokey apse for the high altar with minimal lancet windows. Bringing the altar forward has done something to produce a sense of space, but the east end remains claustrophobic, with the converging arcades adding to the funnel-like effect and concealing the two side chapels. In the south aisle, two large windows have Victorian glass depicting episodes in the history of the abbey in a series of small panels.

The west end, and in particular the south transept, has a pleasingly rugged air, with exposed stone blocks and big blind arches. An elaborate Stuart monument dominates one wall, and there are two much earlier tombs of an abbot and a Knight Templar. The Elizabethan monument in the north transept is without its effigies, but the nine children of the couple commemorated are carved in relief on the front – eight of them earnestly praying and one of the girls apparently taking no interest at all in the proceedings. It is a rare experience to be able to see so much of the interior of the tower, where the unbroken view is made possible by a delicately constructed bell-ringers' platform that makes a floor unnecessary.

The town walk is concluded by returning down Broad Street and turning left at the end into **High Street**. The buildings that face into Broad Street on the opposite side of the road are all distinguished, but none more so than the elegant Angel Inn with its four bow windows. By comparison with the rest of the town, High Street seethes with activity, making a leisurely study of the architecture difficult. The main interest here lies in trying to guess the ages of the shops, since conversion, restoration and general 'doing up' has produced many bland facades that must conceal older interiors, the interesting group on the north corner of Church Street being a case in point. The **Town Hall** is an unassuming heritage centre illustrating the history of the town.

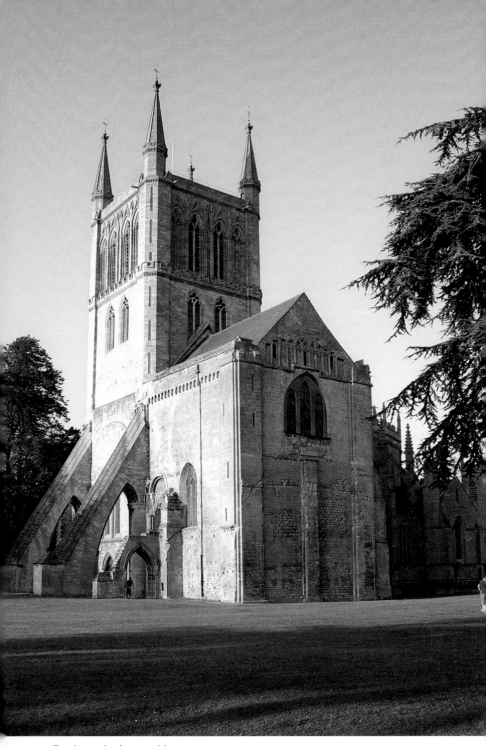

Pershore, the former abbey

Tour 2: South of Pershore: (a tour around Bredon Hill)

From Pershore it is possible to tour some of the best of the Worcestershire countryside, the area that lies around **Bredon Hill** to the south. The hill itself is not dramatic by ordinary standards, being simply a sprawling expanse of higher ground, but in this flat countryside it takes on some significance.

Return to the river bridge and take the minor road for Little Comberton. The contrast between this shaggy, pastoral countryside and the manicured landscape further north is noticeable immediately. There is nothing remarkable at Little Comberton unless it is the line of headstones in the churchyard commemorating generations of the Yeend-Pitcher family, but it is a pleasant place which has absorbed its newer housing well. A few hundred yards on the other side of the village is the signposted start of one of the shorter paths to the top of Bredon Hill, and just beyond it on the left it is possible to catch a glimpse of Bricklehampton Hall, a Victorian mansion designed in an adventurous Italian style, now a nursing home.

Elmley Castle, the next village, can justly claim to be one of the prettiest in Worcestershire. The main street is generous and almost forms a central square, giving the place a natural focus that others lack. A stream runs down one side of the road beneath a row of trees, while on the right is a most interesting range of buildings, including the fine brick Manor Farm and an inspired piece of conversion next door. On a site that used to be a piggery, an E-shaped group of small houses has been constructed round a lawn, fitting admirably into its setting. The cottages next to it represent, quite by chance, the three building styles most commonly found in this area – timber-frame, Cotswold stone and mellow red brick – and the 'square' is closed off by a group of black and white cottages surrounding the Queen Elizabeth. The handsome building opposite the pub is an old barn that once served as a village hall. A right turn at the pub leads you past a splendid five-bay stone house en route for a popular path to the top of Bredon Hill (45 minutes to the top).

The church is pure Cotswold on the outside, crenellated and built of venerable stone. Inside the porch look out for the carved pig and rabbit on the walls. The interior is rather dull, with the exception of some truncated medieval pews in the south aisle and several notable monuments. Of these the most eye-catching is certainly the blatant floor-to-ceiling memorial to the first Earl of Coventry. Apparently it was destined for the family church at Croome, but the second Earl refused to install it there because he could not accept the pedigree which his stepmother had claimed for herself, and included on the monument. The unfortunate Countess managed to get it installed here when she married an Elmley Castle man. Infinitely more distinguished is the chest tomb of Giles Savage, who died in 1631. His effigy lies between those of his father and his wife, who is shown holding a young child. His four sons kneel at his feet. The tomb is a fine, crisp piece of sculpture, marvellously preserved.

A lane opposite the Queen Elizabeth leaves the village, and there follows a pleasant run across high, deserted farmland, surprisingly remote for these parts. The road eventually winds its way to **Ashton under Hill**, a long, straggling village that has grown a great deal in recent years. The old centre is at the southern end.

Beckford, 2m (3km) further on, invites a stop by providing a large and convenient parking place outside the church gate. It is a highly individual place, with a Victorian character promoted by an immense old rectory (now containing a silk-printer's workshop) and a number of harmonious estate cottages. The estate in question belonged to Beckford Hall, once the site of a priory and now converted into flats. The south doorway of the church has been protected by a porch since the fifteenth century, and this has helped to preserve some crudely executed Norman carving on the tympanum. The corresponding work on the north door, though of better workmanship, has suffered a good deal from the weather. The lofty nave retains its Norman walls and two original windows, and the twelfth-century arch at the central tower is finely decorated (note the odd carvings on the north column).

Half a mile (1km) out of Beckford on the Overbury road another path to the summit of Bredon Hill is signposted, and it is about here that the invisible boundary of the Cotswolds is apparently crossed, because **Overbury** is very different from any village seen so far. Whereas Beckford has a casual, workaday air about it, Overbury has all the signs of being a rich man's hobby, and indeed it has belonged to the wealthy Holland-Martin family since the early eighteenth century. John Martin (of Martin's Bank) came to live in the old manor house in 1723, and when it burned down in 1738 he built the present Overbury Court.

At this time the village was something of an industrial centre, with mills producing flour, paper and textiles, but in the late nineteenth century the industries died and some rather eccentric prettification began. The distinguished architect Norman Shaw was called in with instructions to produce instant rustic charm, and the results of his work (a little tongue-in-cheek sometimes) can be seen by walking up the lane to the north of the main road. A turning off the lane provides a vista of the Court's entrance gates and its pedimented facade, set off by some self-conscious cottages at the gate. A little further on is Shaw's superb village hall, and the lane goes on to give access to a mixture of estate cottages and more individual buildings, of which the best is Red House School, a lovely brick mansion with Venetian windows.

From Overbury it is a mere matter of yards to **Kemerton**, most of which lies off the main road to the north and south. It has an appealing centre with an inn and a house next door proclaiming Landaus, Wagonettes and Hunters for Hire. There are no outstanding buildings here, but for the student of domestic architecture Kemerton provides a far greater variety of styles than one would think possible, and a walk along the village lanes is highly recommended.

Bredon gave its name to the Hill and fittingly it is the largest village on the tour. As you approach it from Kemerton, follow the signs for Tewkesbury, cross the railway bridge and then fork right into Church Street, where it is usually possible to park. The church is at the end of this road, distinguished by one of Worcestershire's few rural spires and graced by architecture representing all the best pre-Reformation styles.

There was a very early monastic foundation here, but the present building was begun in the 1180s by some highly superior craftsmen. Their work can be seen immediately at the porch, which is spacious, vaulted and sophisticated in its decoration. The Norman work inside is confined to the short nave area and the western arch of the tower. Different styles are apparent here: the two splayed windows facing each other in the nave are in the early round-arch design, while the tower arch is later, with elaborate capitals and pointed apex. The big south aisle, the Mitton Chapel, is a thirteenth-century addition, notable for two fine windows (now distorted because of subsidence) and three recessed tombs below. Its outstanding feature, however, is a vast marble and alabaster memorial to Sir Giles and Lady Reed, who both died in 1611. They lie in effigy under an architectural canopy with their children kneeling in small 'porches' on each side.

Major alterations took place in the early fourteenth century. The north aisle was added and a spire erected, but the most important development was the new chancel, where there is a canopied tomb of the period and an Easter Sepulchre that has had its crisp carving restored. Note also the decorated coffin lid and the set of heraldic tiles in the sanctuary.

Bredon village has a good deal to offer the visitor prepared to walk round. Just about every style and period of building is represented. In Church Street there are black and white houses of all shapes and sizes, together with the hybrid Fox and Hounds and a splendid Georgian town house. You also pass the backs of the Reed Almhouses, but these are better seen by walking to the fork at the main road and turning right. A little further on are some very expensive modern houses on which opinions will differ, and then a big milestone in obelisk form. Almost next to this is the entrance to Bredon's major attraction, the famous **Tithe Barn**.

In fact it was probably not a tithe barn but a storehouse for the crops of the large Bredon manor. It dates from about 1350, and is built on the same impressive scale as Littleton barn, about 130ft (40m) long and 40ft (12m) wide with nine bays and two wagon porches. There is a fascinating extra feature, though. It is possible to climb a set of stone steps to the reeve's office, which has a projecting window to the front and a balcony on the inside to provide a commanding view of the whole barn. It was not a popular job, and some inducement was provided in the form of a fireplace and a lavatory of simple construction – a hole in a windowsill.

There is a short cut back to Church Street through the churchyard, but before leaving it is possible to glimpse two other substantial buildings near the church. To the north is the former rectory, largely Elizabethan, and to the west the stone manor house is a handsome example of Georgian work.

The return to Pershore is bound to

The tithe barn, Breedon (above and inset)

The River Avon, Breedon

Eckington Bridge, the oldest on the Avon

be something of an anticlimax. Take the B4080 for about 3m (5km) to **Eckington**, another village sideways on to the road and consequently appearing smaller than it is. Double yellow lines discourage stopping, and it is probably better to continue to **Eckington Bridge**, where there is adequate parking space and a chance to relax by the river. The sandstone bridge is rightly famous, being the oldest on the Avon and longer than most packhorse bridges. The fact that it is half a mile from the village is a reminder of the lack of waterside settlements on this stretch of the Avon. The river meanders from Pershore to Bredon and only once skirts a village, at Great Comberton. After a mile the road joins the A4104, and a right turn leads back to Pershore.

The countryside to the west of Pershore makes a pleasant short excursion, beginning on the A4104 (the Upton road) and continuing after 3m (5km) on the lane that leads off to the right after Defford Bridge. The lane runs out of Defford to the north along the edge of a large area of common land which

was once heavily forested. After little more than a mile is the scattered village of **Besford**, situated down an even narrower lane. It has the only remaining timber-framed church in Worcestershire, a fourteenth-century structure with a Victorian chancel extension in stone, and the interior is notable for a rare surviving rood loft. Returning to the main lane and continuing northwards, from the roadside you can see the mixture of buildings that makes up Besford Court, formerly a school and now converted into flats. Basically Tudor, the house was extended during the early years of the twentieth century by the celebrated architect Randall Wells.

At the next crossroads after the Court, turn left and after 2m (3km) watch out for a sharp right-angled turn and the impressive entrance to **Croome Court**. Begun in 1751 for the sixth Earl of Coventry, its design seems to have been shared by several architects – Sanderson Miller, Robert Adam and even Capability Brown have all been suggested. Brown certainly laid out the gardens and possibly planned the nearby church as a carefully sited feature. The house has had a chequered history: since being sold by the Coventry family it has been in turn a school, a Hare Krishna community and a conference centre, and at the time of writing it seems destined to be adapted for flats and houses. Fortunately the National Trust acquired the major part of the Capability Brown parkland, and after restoration the park is open to the public. Past the gate there is a short footpath on the left leading to the church, which is now redundant (a notice on the door gives the current arrangements for obtaining the key). The typically elegant Georgian interior contains some fascinating family tombs.

A further 2m (3km) along the lane is **Pirton Church**, oddly isolated from its village and standing on a hill with a fine view of the Malverns. Its eye-catching feature is the Norman work in the nave (including the doors and ironwork) and a very early font surrounded by medieval tiles. The windows in the chancel survived restoration. As at Dormston there is an intriguing array of timbers at the base of the tower. The lane now passes through Wadborough and joins the B4084 for the return to Pershore.

Places to Visit

IN AND AROUND EVESHAM

Visitor Information
Heritage Centre, Abbey Gate
☎ 01386 446944

Evesham Country Park
WR11 4TP
1m (2km) N of Evesham
☎ 01386 422282
Miniature railway runs through old apple orchards.

Honeybourne Pottery
4m (6km) E of Evesham, in High Street
☎ 01386 832855
Hands-on activities for visitors. Shop.

Bell Tower
Only surviving remains of Evesham Abbey. Tower dates from early 16th century.

Almonry Heritage Centre
Abbey Gate WR11 4BQ
☎ 01386 446944
Rambling building dates from 14th century. Exhibits illustrating history of Evesham and district, including agricultural items and domestic bygones.

Abbey Park and Crown Meadow
Pleasant riverside park and picnic area with children's activities. Boat hire.

Places to Visit

Middle Littleton Tithe Barn (National Trust)

Off B4510/B4085 4m (6km) NE of Evesham
Magnificent manorial barn, fully restored.

Annard Crafts and Woollen Mill

Church Lench, 5m (8km) N of Evesham
Mill open to the public, with shop.

The Fleece Inn

Bretforton, 3m (5km) E of Evesham on B4035
600-year-old pub owned by National Trust, remarkably unaltered.

IN AND AROUND PERSHORE

Visitor Information

Town Hall, High Street
☎ 01386 552482

Pershore Abbey

Tower and east-end only remain after demolition at the Dissolution, but Abbey is still Pershore's parish church. Fine Norman work and memorials beneath tower, superb roof.

Heritage Centre

Town Hall, High Street
☎ 01386 552482
Displays on local history.

Bridge Street

One of the handsomest streets of mixed Georgian buildings in Britain.

Bredon Hill

Various paths to the summit signposted from surrounding roads.

Beckford Silk

The Old Vicarage, Beckford, 9m (15km) S of Pershore off A46
Silk printing workshop open to visitors.

Overbury

7m (11km) S of Pershore at foot of Bredon Hill
Estate cottages and other buildings by famous Victorian architect Norman Shaw.

Bredon Tithe Barn (National Trust)

8m (13km) S of Pershore
14th-century barn, over 130ft (40m) long with reeve's 'office' on first floor.

Eckington Bridge

On B4080, 4m (6km) SE of Pershore
The oldest bridge over the Avon.

Croome Park (National Trust)

Near Pershore
☎ 01905 371006
The oldest bridge over the Avon.

Getting there

Airports
The main airport for this region is Birmingham.

Bus/ Coach
Regular coach services from around the country to the larger towns of the area. Enquiries: National Express 08717 818181 or www.eurolines.co.uk

Car
Access the area from the Motorway system: M40 to the east, M45 to the west and M42 to the north.

Rail
Regular services to a major towns and cities. National rail enquiries ☎ 08457484950 or www.nationalrail.co.uk

Accommodation
Local Tourist Information centres have a booking bureau. See pp 172-173.

Events

GLOUCESTERSHIRE
Gloucester Festivals & Events Guide and also Gloucester Eating Out & Nightlife Guide: call Gloucester Tourist and Information Centre on ☎ 01452 396572.

Cheese Rolling
Coopers Hill, ☎ 01452 863260, **MAY**

SHROPSHIRE

Darwin Festival
various locations around Shrewsbury www.darwinshrewsbury.com, **JAN-FEB**

1960s Transport Day
Severn Valley Railway, Bridgnorth to Kidderminster. Subject to flood damage. ☎ 01299 403816 www.svr.co.uk, **APR**

Shrewsbury Local Food and Drink Fair
☎ 01743 281200, **APR**

Mid-Shropshire Vintage Club Vintage Vehicle Rally
West Mid Showground, Shrewsbury,
SY1 2PF
www.msvintageclub.org.uk, **MAY-JUN**

Much Wenlock Festival
various locations around Much Wenlock www.muchwenlockfestival.co.uk, **MAY-JUN**

Church Stretton Walking Festival
various locations around the area ☎ 01694 723600 www.churchstrettonwalkingfestival.co.uk, **JUN**

West Mid Show
The West Mid Show Ground, Shrewsbury SY1 2PF ☎ 0870 957 6444, www.westmidshow.co.uk, **JUN**

Opera in the Square
The Square, Shrewsbury SY1 1LH ☎ 01743 281 281 www.shrewsburysummer.co.uk, **JUL**

Oswestry Food and Drink Festival
various locations around Oswestry ☎ 01691 655615 www.oswestryfoodfestival.co.uk, **JUL**

Shrewsbury Flower Show
The Quarry, Shrewsbury
01743 234050
www.shrewsburyflowershow.org.uk,
AUG

Church Stretton Food Fayre
various locations around Church
Stretton
☎ 01694 751245, www.foodfayre.org,
AUG

County of Salop Steam Engine Rally
Onslow Park, Shrewsbury SY3 5EE
01743 792 731
www.shrewsburysteamrally.co.uk, **AUG**

WARWICKSHIRE

Shakespeare's Birthday
Stratford-upon-Avon, **APR**

Living Shakespeare
Stratford-upon-Avon, **MAY**

Rose Festival
Coughton Court, Alcester, **JUN**

Warwick Carnival
Various venues, Warwick, **JUN**

Grand Summer Concert
Warwick Castle, Warwick, **JUL**

Rose Festival
Coughton Court, Alcester, **JUL**

Royal International Agricultural Show
Stoneleigh, **JUL**

Summer of Jousting, Archery Falconry & Combat
Warwick Castle, Warwick, **JUL-SEP**

Horticultural Annual Flower Show & Craft Fair
Warwick, Aug Bank Holiday Weekend.

Apple Day & Harvest Fair

Mary Ardens House, Stratford-upon-Avon, **OCT**

Midlands Model Engineering Exhibition
Warwickshire Exhibition Centre, Leamington Spa, **OCT**

Stratford Mop Fair
Stratford-upon-Avon, **OCT**

Victorian Christmas Evening
Warwick, **NOV**

WORCESTERSHIRE

British Asparagus Festival
Including Festival weekend at The Fleece, Bretforton.
01386 565373
www.britishasparagusfestival.org, **APR**

Spring Fayre
Croome Park, Worcester, **MAY**

Three Counties Show
01684 584900, www.threecounties.co.uk, **JUN**

Evesham Morris, Medieval & Cider Festival
01386 565518 www.worcestershires-heritage-garden.org, **JUN**

Harvington Festival
Harvington Hall, Kidderminster, **JUN**

Alpine Society National Show
Pershore College, Pershore, **JUL**

Gt Comberton Flower Show
Brailes Orchard, Gt Comberton, , 01386 711009, **AUG**

Three Choirs Festival
Various venues, Gloucester, Hereford or Worcester, **AUG**

CAMRA Beer festival
Pitchcroft
www.worcesterbeerfest.org.uk, **AUG**

Heritage Open Day
Croome Park , Severn Stoke, **SEP**

Heritage Open Day
Harvington Hall , Kidderminster, **SEP**

Worcester Christmas Fayre
☎ 01905 726311,
www.visitworcester.com

Farmers' Markets

GLOUCESTERSHIRE

Berkeley Farmers' Market
Every 3rd Sat of the month, Town Hall,
9am–12.30pm.

☎ 01453 890383 *Gloucester*
• The Cross, every Fri
• Kings Sq., every Sat
  (Cherry & White Market)
• Westgate Medieval Fayre. The city
  centre is changed into a medieval
  village for a day in June.
  ☎ 01452 412828

Tewkesbury Farmers' Market
Every 2nd Thu of the month, Cascades
Leisure Centre car park, 9am–2.30pm.
Refreshments are available at the
Farmers' Market.
Ample parking is available nearby.

SHROPSHIRE

Church Stretton
2nd & 4th Fri of the month. Market Square
☎ 01694 722113

Craven Arms
1st Sat of the month. Shropshire Hills
Discovery Centre, ☎ 01588 676000

Much Wenlock
1st & 3rd Fri of the month Guildhall
☎ 01952 727509

Shrewsbury
1st Fri of the month, The Square,
☎ 01746 785185

WARWICKSHIRE

Kenilworth
Abbey End, 2nd Sat of the month,
9am–2pm

Leamington Spa
Pump Room Gardens, 4th Sat of the
month , 9am–2pm

Stratford upon Avon
Rother Street, 1st and 3rd Sat of the
month, 9am–2pm

Warwick
The Market Square, 3rd Fri of the month
9am–2pm

WORCESTERSHIRE

Crown Gate Market
Worcester
☎ 01895 639912

Malvern Farmers' Market
Malvern
☎ 07795 656148

Pershore Plum Fayre & Farmers'
Market
August
☎ 01386 556591

Worcester Farmers' Market
Worcester
☎ 07795 656148

Leisure Centres

GLOUCESTERSHIRE

Gloucester

Beaufort Sports Centre
Windsor Drive, Tuffley GL4 0RT
☎ 01452 303256

Brockworth Sports Centre
Mill Lane, Brockworth GL3 4QF
☎ 01452 863518

Churchdown Sports Centre
Winston Road, Churchdown GL3 2RB
☎ 01452 855994

GL1 Gloucester Leisure Centre
Bruton Way GL1 1DT
☎ 01452 396666

Riverside Sports & Leisure Club
St. Oswalds Road GL1 2TF
☎ 01452 413214

Sir Thomas Rich's Sports Centre
Oakleaze, Longlevens GL2 0LF
☎ 01452 338439

The Warehouse Climbing Centre

The Warehouse Health Club
Parliament Street GL1 1HY
☎ 01452 302351

Tewkesbury

Cascades
Oldbury Road GL20 5LR
☎ 01684 293740

Tewkesbury Sports Centre
Ashchurch Road, Newtown GL20 8DF
☎ 01684 293953

SHROPSHIRE

Bewdley

Bewdley Leisure Centre
Stourport Road DY12 1BL
☎ 01299 402595

Bridgnorth

Bridgnorth Sports & Leisure Centre
Northgate WV16 4ER
☎ 01746 761541

Severn Centre
Bridgnorth Road
Highley
WV16 6JG
☎ 01746 860000

Shrewsbury

London Road Sports Centre
London Road SY2 6PR
☎ 01743 232098

Radbrook Elite Health & Leisure Club
Radbrook Road SY3 9BQ
☎ 01743 361253

Grange Sports Centre
Mount Pleasant Road SY1 3LP
☎ 01743 241397

Roman Road Sports Centre
Longden Road SY3 9DW
☎ 01743 351916

Monkmoor Recreation Centre
Racecourse Crescent SY2 5BP
☎ 01743 361088

WARWICKSHIRE

Alcester

The Greig Centre
Kinwarton Road B49 6AD
☎ 01789 400073

Kenilworth

Castle Farm Recreation Centre
Fishponds Road CV8 1EY
☎ 01926 850550

Leamington Spa

Sydenham Sports Centre
Campion High School, Sydenham Drive
CV31 1QH
☎ 01926 330668

Newbold Comyn Leisure Centre
Newbold Terrace East, Newbold Comyn
CV32 4EW
☎ 01926 882083

Whitnash Community Hall
Acre Close, Whitnash CV31 2ND
☎ 01926 425219

Stratford-Upon-Avon

Stratford Community Sports Centre
Alcester Road CV37 9DH
☎ 01789 267661

Warwick

Ardencote Manor Leisure Club
Lye Green Road Claverdon CV35 8HJ
☎ 01926 843872

St. Nicholas Park Leisure Centre
Banbury Road CV34 4QY
☎ 01926 495353

WORCESTERSHIRE

Droitwich

Droitwich Spa Leisure Centre
Briar Mill WR9 0RZ
☎ 01905 771212

Evesham

Worcestershire Cricket Centre
Victoria Avenue WR11 4QH
☎ 01386 45074

Hartlebury

Parkwood Leisure Ltd
Little BowbrookWalton Road
DY10 4JA
☎ 01299 253400

Malvern

Banana Fitness
Priory Road WR14 3DS
☎ 01684 562592

Pershore

Pershore Leisure Centre
King Georges Way WR10 1QU
☎ 01386 552346

Worcester

Nunnery Wood Sports Complex
Spetchley Road WR5 2NL
☎ 01905 357842

Perdiswell Leisure Centre
Bilford Road WR3 8DX
☎ 01905 457189

St. John's Sports Centre
Swanpool Walk WR2 4EL
☎ 01905 429900

Sport Dyson Perrins
Yates Hay Road WR14 1WD
☎ 01684 572645

Nature Reserves

GLOUCESTERSHIRE

Gloucester City Council manages three areas in the city

Alney Island
Important wetland habitat for flora and fauna

Hucclecote Hay Meadows
Traditional meadowland, access from Lobley's Drive, Hucclecote

Quedgeley Nature Reserve
Impressive list of fauna access on Curtis Hayward Drive, off Severn Vale Drive

Robinswood Hill Country Park
2 mlnutes south of Gloucester, off the A4173.
250 acres of countryside with pleasant walks & views. Waymarked nature, geology & horse trails. Gloucestershire Wildlife Trust visitor centre
☎ 01452 38333, exhibition & gift shop open 9am–5pm. A guided walks programme is also available. Rare breeds farm.
☎ 01452 304779
Open all year, daily. Closed at dusk, check the times on the gate. Admission free.

For more information contact:

Gloucestershire Wildlife Trust
Robinswood Hill Country Park
Reservoir Road
Gloucester
GL4 6SX
☎ 01452 383333

SHROPSHIRE

Chelmarsh
6km south of Bridgnorth, off the B4555.

Comley Quarry
6km north east of Church Stretton.

Cramer Gutter
Part of the much longer Catherton Common, 5km north west of Cleobury Mortimer.

Monkmoor Pool
On edge of Shrewsbury town at end of Monkmoor Road, easily seen from the A49 bypass.

The Ercall
South of the M54 and Wellington.

WARWICKSHIRE

Warwickshire Wildlife Trust
Brandon Marsh Nature Centre, Brandon Lane, Coventry CV3 3GW
☎ 024 7630 2912
enquiries@wkwt.org.uk
www.warwickshire-wildlife-trust.org.uk

WORCESTERSHIRE

Worcester Wildlife Trust
Lower Smite Farm, Smite Hill
Hindlip, Worcester, WR3 8SZ
☎ 01905 754919
enquiries@wkwt.org.uk
www.warwickshire-wildlife-trust.org.uk

Sports Facilities

Golf

For information on local golf facilities go to www.theinternetgolfclub.com.

Horse Riding

There are plenty of opportunities to ride throughout the areas covered by this guide; we suggest you look up the various websites for the counties for more information.

www.gloucestershire.gov.uk
www.warks.co.uk/horse-riding
www.shropshireriding.co.uk

River Cruises

GLOUCESTERSHIRE

English Holiday Cruises Ltd.

2; 4 or 6 day cruises on Britain's biggest riverboat hotel, (The *Oliver Cromwell*), or on the *Edward Elgar*, between Bewdley and Sharpness (south of Slimbridge).
☎ 0845 601 7895

SHROPSHIRE

Shrewsbury River Cruises

Victoria Quay, Shrewsbury
☎ 01244 325394

WARWICKSHIRE

Avon Boating

Stratford-upon-Avon
☎ 01787 267073

Bancroft Cruises

Holiday Inn Hotel
Bridge Foot
Stratford upon Avon
CV37 6YR
☎ 01789 269669
captain@bancroftcruisers.co.uk

WORCESTERSHIRE

Avon Leisure Cruises

Avon Cottage
Mill Bank
Fladbury
Pershore
WR10 2QA
☎ 07774 653112
enquiries@avonleisurecruises.co.uk

Worcester River Cruises

37 The Tything, Worcester, WR1 1JL
☎ 01905 611060
www.worcesterrivercruises.co.uk

Tourist Information Centres

GLOUCESTERSHIRE

Gloucester Tourist Information

28 Southgate Street, Gloucester,
GL1 2DP
☎ 01452 396572

Gloucester Tourist Information Service

Shire Hall, Westgate Street

Gloucester, GL1 2TG
☎ 01452 425673

Tewkesbury Heritage & Visitor Centre

100 Church Street, Tewkesbury
GL20 5AB
☎ 01684 855040

SHROPSHIRE

Bridgnorth Visitor Information Centre
The Library, Listley Street, Bridgnorth, WV16 4AW
☎ 01746 763257

Church Stretton Visitor Information Centre
Church Street, Church Stretton, SY6 6DG
☎ 01694 723133

Craven Arms Visitor Information
Centre School Road, Craven Arms, Shropshire, SY7 9RS
☎ 01588 676000

Ironbridge Visitor Information Centre
The Tollhouse, Ironbridge, Telford, TF8 7JS
☎ 01952 884391

Much Wenlock Visitor Information Centre
The Museum, High Street, Much Wenlock, TF13 6HR
☎ 01952 727679

Shrewsbury Visitor Information Centre
The Music Hall, The Square, Shrewsbury, SY1 1LH
☎ 01743 281200

Telford Visitor Information Centre
The Telford Shopping Centre, Telford, TF3 4BX
☎ 01952 230032

WARWICKSHIRE

Stratford upon Avon
Bridgefoot, Stratford upon Avon, CV37 6GW
☎ 0870 1607930

Warwick
The Court House, Jury Street, Warwick CV34 4EW
☎ 01926 492212

Leamington Spa
The Royal Pump Rooms, The Parade Leamington Spa, CV32 4AD
☎ 0870 1607930

Kenilworth
(Within Kenilworth Library)
11 Smalley Place sKenilworth, CV8 1QG
☎ 01926 748900

WORCESTERSHIRE

Heart of England Tourism
Lark Hill Road, Worcester
WR5 2EZ, ☎ 01905 761100

Pershore Visitor Information Centre
Town Hall, 34 High Street, Pershore WR10 1DS
☎ 01386 556591

Upton-upon-Severn
4 High Street, Upton-upon-Severn Worcester, WR8 0HB
☎ 01684 594200

Worcester
The Guildhall, Worcester, WR1 2EZ
☎ 01905 726311

Malvern
21 Church Street, Malvern, WR14 2AA
☎ 01684 892289

Index

A

Abbey Park and Crown Meadow 164
Abdon 29
Abdon Burf 29
Alcester 131, 133, 136-37, 141-42, 144-45
Alderminster 128
All Saints' Church 120
Almonry Heritage Centre 147, 149, 164
Alveley 40
Annard Craftsand Woollen Mill 165
Anne Hathaway's Cottage 133, 143
Areley Kings 44
Arley Arboretum 52
Ashleworth 92
Aston Cantlow 141
Atcham 16, 34
Attingham Park 17, 34
Avon boat trips 144
Avoncroft Museum of Historic Buildings 49, 53

B

Barton 129
Battlefield Church 35
Bear Steps, Shrewsbury 11, 13, 34
Beckford 160
Beckford Silk 165
Bell Tower 148, 151, 164
Benthall 22
Benthall Hall 22
Berkeley 102
Berkeley Castle 94, 105
Besford 163
Bewdley 39-43, 52-3
Bewdley Museum 52
Bidford-on-Avon 137
Billesley 141
Binton 137
Black Bear Inn 89
Blackfriars Priory, Gloucester 104
Blists Hill 21, 36
Bodenham Arboretumand Earth Centre 52
Bouldon 28
brass foundry 42, 52
Brass Rubbing Centre 144
Bredon Hill 159-60, 165
Bredon Tithe Barn 165
Bretforton 132
Bridge Street 149, 156, 165
Bridgnorth 32
Brockhampton Estate 80
Broseley 20-22, 36
Buildwas 18-19, 21, 36

Buildwas Abbey 18-19, 36
Bungo's Barn 145

C

Castle, Kenilworth 120
Chaddesley Corbett 49, 51
Charlecote 118
Charlecote Park 144
Chateau Impney 50, 53
Clee St Margaret 29
Cleeve Prior 129
Clifford Chambers 129
Coalbrookdale 20-21, 29, 35-36
Coalport China Museum 22
Coleham Pumping Station 34
Compton Verney 144
Coughton Court 133, 136, 144
Croome Court 163
Croome Park 103, 165
Cropthorne 149

D

Deerhurst 90, 103
Deerhurst Church 103
Diddlebury 27, 28
Diglis Canal Basin 80
Droitwich 48-50, 53
Droitwich Heritage Centre 50
Dudmaston Hall 38

E

Eastgate Viewing Chamber 104
Easthope 25-26
Eastnor 77
Eastnor Castle 76, 81
Eaton-under-Heywood 28
Eckington 163, 165
Eckington Bridge 163, 165
Edward Jenner Museum 105
Elgar Birthplace Museum 80
Evesham 146-51, 154, 164-65
Evesham Country Park 164

F

Fladbury 149
Fleece Inn 165
Framilode 101
Frampton-on-Severn 101
Funky Monkeys 121

G

George MarshallMedical Museum 80
Glasshampton monastery 45
Gloucester 82-83, 90-105
Gloucester Antiques Centre 105
Gloucester Cathedral 103
Gloucester City Museum & Art Gallery 104
Gloucester Docks 98-99, 104-05
Gloucester Folk Museum 104
Gloucester Guildhall 104
Glover's Needle 57, 63
Great Alne 141
Great Malvern 68, 69, 77, 81
Great Witley 45
Greyfriars 61, 67, 79
Guildhall, Worcester 55, 65, 79

H

Hagley Hall 52
Hall's Croft 125, 143
Hanbury Hall 53
Hanley Castle 78
Hartlebury Castle 48, 52
Harvard House 125, 143
Harvington Hall 47-9, 52
Haselor 141
Hatton Country World 121
Hatton Locks 121
Haughmond Abbey 35
Heath 28
Henley-in-Arden 137, 139, 141
Hereford and Worcester County Museum 52
Herefordshire Beacon 81
Heritage Motor Centre 121
Hidcote Manor Garden 145
Hill Close Victorian Gardens 121
Holt 45
Holy Trinity Church 124, 143
Honeybourne 132
Honeybourne Pottery 164
Hoo Mill 136
House of the Tailor of Gloucester 104
Hughley 25

I

Ilmington 128
Inkberrow 153
Ironbridge 16, 18, 20-1, 30, 35-36
Ironbridge Gorge 18, 20, 35

J

Jackfield Tile Museum 22
Jephson Gardens 108-09, 110, 120
Jinny Ring Craft Centre 53
John MooreCountryside Museum 103
John Moore Museum 89
Joseph Arch 118

K
Kemerton 160
Kenilworth 106-07, 110-13, 120
Kidderminster 38, 40-1, 45,
    48, 52
Kiftsgate Court Gardens 128, 145
Kinwarton 136

L
Leam Boat Centre 120
Leamington Spa 106, 108, 111
Little Malvern Priory 77, 81
Llanthony Secunda Priory 104
Lord Leycester Hospital 115-16,
    121
Lower Quinton128

M
Malvern Hills 68, 71, 73-4, 81
Malvern Museum 81
Malvern Showground 81
Malvern Theatres 69, 81
Market Hall, Shrewsbury 13, 34
Marlcliff 129
Martin Hussingtree 50
Mary Arden's House 140, 143
Middle Littleton 132
Middle Littleton Tithe Barn 165
Minsterworth 101
Morville Hall 29
Much Wenlock 18, 22-4, 28-9,
    36, 37
Much Wenlock Priory 24
Museum of Iron 21, 35

N
National Agricultural Centre 110
National Waterways Museum 83,
    98, 104
Newbold Comyn 109-10, 120
Newbold on Stour 128
Newland Churchand
    Almshouses 81
New Place and Nash's House 143
Nordybank 29

O
Offenham 132
Ombersley 48, 51
Overbury 160, 165

P
Pebworth 132
Pershore 146, 149, 156-59, 161,
    163, 164-65
Pershore Abbey 165
Preston on Stour 127
Priory Park 121

Pump House Environment Centre
    80

Q
Quarry, Shrewsbury 16, 34

R
Ragley Hall 136, 145
Redwings Rescue Centre 145
Robinswood Hill Country Park
    & Rare Breeds Centre 104
Roman Alcester 145
Rous Lench 152-53, 155
Rowley's House, Shrewsbury
    16-7, 34
Royal Pump Rooms 120
Royal Shakespeare Theatre 124,
    143
Royal Worcester Porcelain 57
Royal WorcesterVisitor Centre 79
Rushbury 27-8

S
Sayers Almshouses 42
Severn Vale 82, 100
Severn Valley Railway 40, 52-3
Shakespeare's Birthplace 127,
    143
Shakespeare Monument 124
Shakespearience 144
Sherbourne 117
Shipton Hall 29, 37
Shottery 133
Shrewsbury 10-17, 24, 34-5
Shrewsbury Abbey 15
Soldiers of Gloucestershire
    Museum 105
Spetchley Park Gardens 80
St Ann's Well 73, 81
St Augustine's Farm 105
St Chad's Church, Shrewsbury
    15, 34
St James's City Farm 105
St John's House Museum 121
St Mary's Church, Shrewsbury
    13, 34, 37
St Nicholas Park 112, 117, 121
Stone House Cottage Gardens 52
Stoneleigh 110
Stoneleigh Abbey 110, 120
Stourport 40-1, 43-4, 48, 53
Stourport Canal Basins 53
St Peter's Church 140, 145
Stratford-upon-Avon 122-23,
    126-27, 144
Stratford-upon-Avon Canal 144
Stratford Greenway 144
Stroudwater Canal 101

St Swithun's Church 79
St Wulfstan's RomanCatholic
    Church 81

T
Temple Grafton 137
Tewkesbury 83-88, 90, 103
Tewkesbury Abbey 86, 88, 103
Tewkesbury Town Museum 103
The Castle, Shrewsbury 31,
    34, 37
The Commandery 61, 67, 79
Tiltridge Vineyard 103
Tontine Hotel 44, 53
Tudor House Heritage Centre 79

U
Upper Arley 40, 41
Upper Quinton 128
Upton-upon-Severn 82, 84

V
Viroconium 17, 34

W
Warwick 106, 109, 112-13, 115-
    18, 121
Warwick Boats 121
Warwick Castle 115, 121
Warwickshire Museum 121
Welford on Avon 129
Wellesbourne Watermill 145
Wenlock Edge 24, 37
West Midland Safari Park 40
West Midlands Safari and
    Leisure Park 53
Weston 129
Wharf House, Gloucester 105
Wildfowl and Wetlands Centre
    102, 105
Wilmcote 140
Wimpstone 128
Witley Court 39, 44, 45, 46, 53
Wixford 137
Wootton Wawen 140
Worcester 38, 44, 48-50, 52-8,
    60-1, 63-68, 78-80
Worcester Cathedral 58, 60, 79
Worcester Porcelain Museum 80
Worcestershire Beacon 81
Worcestershire County Museum 48
Worcestershire History Centre 80
Worcester Three Choirs Festival
    80
Worcester Woods Country Park
    80
Wroxeter Vineyard 34
Wyre Forest Visitor Centre 53

Published by
Landmark Publishing Ltd,
Ashbourne Hall, Cokayne Ave, Ashbourne, Derbyshire DE6 1EJ England
Tel: (01335) 347349 Fax: (01335) 347303 e-mail: landmark@clara.net
Website www.landmarkpublishing.co.uk

ISBN 978-1-84306-390-2

© **Lawrence Garner 2008**

British Library Cataloguing in Publication Data: a catalogue record for this
book is available from the British Library.

Print: Cromwell Press, Trowbridge
Design: Mark Titterton
Cartography: Mark Titterton

Front cover: Warkwick Castle
Back cover top: Shakespeare's birthplace, Stratford-upon-Avon
(www.enjoywarwickshire.com)
Back cover Bottom: Gloucester Cathedral (Gloucester City Council)
Page 2: Fish Street, Shrewsbury

Picture Credits

Landmark Publishing gratefully acknowlege the supply of various photographs
for this guide to Severn and Avon; including

Gloucester City Council – www.visitgloucester.info – pages 6, 82, 87, 91, 95 , 99 inset
and cover back-bottom

Destination Worcestershire – www.visitworcestershire.org
© **Worcestershire County Council** – pages 54, 74 bottom

Warwickshire – www.enjoywarwickshire.com – pages 7 inset, 111 top, 122, 123, 126 and
cover back-top

Ironbridge Gorge Museum Trust – page 31 top-right

Shutterstock – page 7 David Hughes and page 87 Daniel Gale

Royal Shakespeare Company – www.rsc.org.uk – page 126 top

Mark Titterton – pages 2, 10, 11, 14 and 15

All other photography by Lindsey Porter